PRAISE FOR *TORN FROM THE WORLD*

"John Gibler's powerful recounting of the forced disappearance of Andrés Tzompaxtle Tecpile unearths the brutal machinery of state-sanctioned torture and terrorism in Mexico today. It is also a deeply lyrical story of survival against the odds, enabled by communities of resistance and solidarity. This book must provoke an outcry. We cannot know this story and see the world in the same way."

—Sujatha Fernandes, author *of Curated Stories:*
The Uses and Misuses of Storytelling

"Once in a long while a brilliant writer happens on a story he was born to tell—a story that in its stark and unremitting horror gives us a glimpse of the world as it is, unvarnished and unredeemed. John Gibler is such a writer and *Torn From the World* such a story. A wrenching, astonishing tale, brilliantly told."

—Mark Danner, author of *Spiral* and
The Massacre at El Mozote

"There are things that we would rather not know. Those are precisely the things that John Gibler investigates and comes back to tell us. Here he dwells on the unconscionable and methodic tortures to which the Mexican State submitted Andrés Tzompaxtle Tecpile. But, also, he tells the story of how this man didn't let himself be erased by his torturers, preserving his humanity. *Torn from the World* is the product of a thorough investigation and it is written with rage and humility at the same time. This is the work of one of the most important journalists of our time."

—Yuri Herrera, author of *Signs Preceding the End of the World*

"Not since Rodolfo Walsh's classic *Operation Massacre* have I read a work of political and literary journalism as inventive and urgent as John Gibler's *Torn from the World*. With courage, empathy, and clear-sightedness, Gibler tackles questions most journalists won't go near. How to capture in language and via memory practices—torture and disappearance—designed to destroy meaning and erase the past? How to write without complicity or exploitation? How to listen, and to fight? How to take sides with truth? *Torn from the World* is at once gripping and profound. It is, to borrow Gibler's phrase, an 'insurgent embrace,' hopeful and defiant, a work of outrage and of love."

—Ben Ehrenreich, author of *The Way to the Spring: Life and Death in Palestine*

"At once harrowing and humane, John Gibler's wonderful new book *Torn from the World* shines a light on the darkest corners of the Mexican justice system. We cannot turn away from what we see there. This is a brave, daring book, equal in every way to the extraordinary life it documents."

—Daniel Alarcón, author of *At Night We Walk in Circles*

"John Gibler's brilliantly written story of the abduction, disappearance, and torture of Andrés Tzompaxtle Tecpile assembles the personal testimonies of Tzompaxtle, his wife, and his brother, and interviews with journalists, a former guerrilla leader, and human rights advocates to provide an approximation to the truth. Tzompaxtle is but one of the thousands of Mexicans who have been disappeared in recent years by the State, the cartels or a combination of the two. Writing against a proliferation of semi-official reports and denials claiming truth and that raise questions about the veracity of the testimonies and interviews, Gibler faces the phantom of writing violence: the violence one exerts when writing about violence. Can one avoid writing violence? Can memory provide evidence beyond its inevitable subjective anchorings? Anticipating these questions, Gibler's story of Tzompaxtle's disappearance includes theoretical reflections on memory and violence. In these times when truth is relativized for the sake of political expediency, Gibler's is a sobering account that provides readers with the materials from which he elaborates his story of Tzompaxtle. This book offers an implicit response to the denigration of journalism, hence of truth-telling."

—José Rabasa, author of *Writing Violence on the Northern Frontier*

"John Gibler has produced a giant of a book. A combination of a political thriller, personal testimony, interviews, and deep, insightful reflection, *Torn from the World* is a work full of pain. It is also charged with hope—a hope born of the struggle against systemic violence, and of the struggle to survive and to live in a better world, one of equality for all."

—Joseph Nevins, author of *Dying to Live: A Story of U.S. Immigration in an Age of Global Apartheid*

"In this great work of literary journalism we come to know a life of vertigo in a Mexico still more opaque and unjust than the one we see in the newspapers and social media. This is the shadow Mexico where armed struggle and fierce repression wage a decades-long battle. . . . *Torn from the World* proves that John Gibler views writing as a form of dissent, of going against the grain. It also shows, through the story of an impossible escape, that in the Mexico of the shadows, every once in a while, one finds a bit of light."

—Diego Osorno, *Más por más*

"John Gibler has written a raw and forceful portrait to show the extremes of violence and torture."

—Juan Carlos Talavera, *Excelsior*

"With rigor and imagination in equal measure, John Gibler mixes literary metaphor with narrative journalism, testimony with the theoretical essay, the open-ended interview with critical reflection."

—Andrés Fabián Henao, *Palabras al Margen*

"Beyond the reporting or the mere description of the events, *Torn from the World* by John Gibler is a conversation from the shadows of clandestinity that seeks to step away from the power relations that characterize the journalist's labor. . . . Here one finds a bone-chilling testimony from the school of pain to which men and women with ideals and a thirst for justice are submitted in a country like [Mexico], dominated by autocrats and criminals disguised as public officials."

—Lobsang Castañeda, *Revista Leemás*

"Andrés Tzompaxtle Tecpile, a member of a guerrilla group in the Mexican state of Guerrero, was abducted by the Mexican military one evening in October 1996, held for four months, and brutally tortured. Gibler, the author of the shattering *I Couldn't Even Imagine That They Would Kill Us* (2017), presents another devastating but necessary book. Reading this in light of the confirmation of the latest director of the CIA, Gina

Haspel, who oversaw 'enhanced interrogation techniques' in an earlier CIA position, is especially poignant in that this is a powerful reminder of the dreadful cost the use of torture entails, and of the U.S.' role in perpetuating torture on the American continents. Gibler's interviews with Tzompaxtle Tecpile provide the marrow for a carefully researched, meticulously constructed, and often excruciating narrative. While honoring Tzompaxtle Tecpile's story, Gibler honors the reader's intelligence, nimbly deconstructing the roots and the legacy of torture. This is an important look at the price exacted by the legitimatizing of state-sponsored violence and the concealment of the truth about such operations, and their disastrous consequences for everyone."

—Sara Martinez, *Booklist*, Starred Review

CHOSEN ONE OF THE BEST BOOKS OF 2017
BY *PUBLISHERS WEEKLY*

"Journalist Gibler's investigative prowess yields a book that uses a chorus of voices—eyewitness accounts of the students and others at the scene—to add depth and clarity to the Sept. 26, 2014, massacre of students in the city of Iguala, Mexico, that left six people dead, 40 wounded, and 43 students missing who have yet to be seen since. It's an unforgettable reconstruction of a national tragedy."

—*Publishers Weekly*, Starred Review

"[A] raw and vulnerable glimpse into the violence that continues to affect parts of Mexico. . . . Readers interested in learning more about crime and corruption in Mexico, especially from the point of view of the victims, will want to read this book."

—*Library Journal*

"This is an essential work of exacting, caring, and memorializing reportage."

—*Booklist*, Starred Review

"In Mexico, John Gibler's book has been recognized as a journalistic masterpiece, an instant classic, and the most powerful indictment available of the devastating state crime committed against the 43 disappeared Ayotzinapa students in Iguala. This meticulous, choral re-creation of the events of that night is brilliantly vivid and alive, it will terrify and inspire you and shatter your heart."

—Francisco Goldman, author of *The Interior Circuit: A Mexico City Chronicle*

"The hideous Ayotzinapa atrocity reveals with vivid horror how Mexico is being destroyed by the U.S.-based 'drug war' and its tentacles, penetrating deeply into the security system, business, and government, and strangling what is decent and hopeful in Mexican society. Gibler's remarkable investigations lift the veil from these terrible crimes and call for concerted action to extirpate the rotten roots and open the way for recovery from a grim fate."

—Noam Chomsky

"A powerful and searing account of a devastating atrocity. Gibler's innovative style takes us on a compelling journey through a landscape of terror and brutality against those whose only crime was to demand the freedom to think."

—Brad Evans, columnist on violence for the *New York Times* and the *Los Angeles Review of Books*

"We are fortunate to now have in English, John Gibler's courageous account and oral history of the 2014 atrocity in Mexico in which 43 students vanished from the face of the earth and remain absent, while six more people (three of them students) were found dead, one of them mutilated. The U.S. 'war on drugs' has unleashed decades of unimaginable and hideous terrorism in Mexico, just as the 'war on terror' is doing in the Middle East. The cruel viciousness of Ayotzinapa, with the 48 families of all the disappeared, murdered, and critically wounded students insisting on answers from the Mexican government, opens the door to a powerful resistance movement, which also requires U.S. citizens to insist on ending the U.S. war against the Mexican people, which began in the 1820s and has never abated."

—Roxanne Dunbar-Ortiz, author of *An Indigenous Peoples'
History of the United States* and the forthcoming
The US-Mexican War, 1846–1848

TORN
FROM THE
WORLD

A Guerrilla's Escape
From a Secret Prison in Mexico

John Gibler

City Lights Books | Open Media Series

Originally published in Spanish as *Tzompaxtle: La fuga de un guerrillero* by Tusquets Editores (Mexico) in 2014.

Cover design by: Victor Mingovits, victor@mingovits.com

The Open Media Series is edited by Greg Ruggiero.

Library of Congress Cataloging-in-Publication Data
Names: Gibler, John, author.
Title: Torn from the world : a guerrilla's escape from a secret prison in
  Mexico / John Gibler.
Other titles: Tzompaxtle. English
Description: San Francisco, CA : City Lights Books, [2018] | Series: Open
  media series | "Translated, revised and expanded from the Spanish original
  by John Gibler." | Includes bibliographical references.
Identifiers: LCCN 2018007078 (print) | LCCN 2018027884 (ebook) |
  ISBN 9780872867833 | ISBN 9780872867529
Subjects: LCSH: Tzompaxtle Tecpile, Andrés—Interviews. | Guerrero
(Mexico :
  State)—Underground movements. | Ejército Popular Revolucionario
(Mexico)
  | Disappeared persons—Mexico—Interviews. | Victims of state-sponsored
  terrorism—Mexico—Interviews.
Classification: LCC F1286 (ebook) | LCC F1286 .G5313 2018 (print) |
DDC
  972/.73—dc23
LC record available at https://lccn.loc.gov/2018007078

City Lights Books are published at the City Lights Bookstore
261 Columbus Avenue, San Francisco, CA 94133
www.citylights.com

CONTENTS

For Andrés Tzompaxtle Tecpile:
More than an effort to tell your story,
this is an effort to honor your story.

For all who struggle such that there be no
more stories like this.

In memoriam: Edwin B. Allaire (1930–2013)

And, unfortunately,
pain expands in the world all the time,
it grows thirty minutes per second, step by step,
and the nature of pain, is twice the pain
and the condition of misery, carnivorous, voracious,
is twice the pain . . .

     —César Vallejo, "The Nine Monsters"

In a work of nonfiction we almost never know the truth of
what happened.

     —Janet Malcolm, *The Silent Woman*

It's more than true, it actually happened.

     —Gogol Bordello, "Inmigraniada"

Art, he said, forms part of the particular history long before forming part of art history as such. Art, he said, is the
particular history. It is the only particular history possible.
It is the particular history and at the same time the womb
of the particular history. And what is the womb of the particular history, I asked. Immediately afterward I thought he
would respond: art. I also thought, and this was a courteous
thought, that we were drunk and it was time to go home.
But my friend said: the womb of the particular history is
the secret history.

     —Roberto Bolaño, "The Dentist"

We only wanted the opportunity to tell a little bit of all the
truth, of so much truth that exists.

     —Estela Ríos González, interview

PROLOGUE TO THE ENGLISH TRANSLATION

TORN FROM THE WORLD IS a book about Andrés Tzompaxtle Tecpile and his struggle to survive torture and forced disappearance, about the logics, techniques, and infrastructure of torture and forced disappearance, about social struggle and armed anti-colonial insurgency, and about writing. While I worked on the first Spanish edition of this book between 2011 and 2013, I was terrified to see how the State practice of forced disappearance had been incorporated into the tactics used by the entrepreneurs of kidnapping and extortion, how there was a kind of steroid-fueled resurgence of forced disappearances happening under the guise of the so-called War on Drugs. Those forced disappearances continue unabated. No one knows how many people are now disappeared in Mexico, but the only and almost certainly understated official federal number is more than 30,000.

Some six months after this book's original February 2014 Spanish-language publication in Mexico, more than 100 municipal, state, and federal police as well as non-uniformed armed men attacked the students of Ayotzinapa in Iguala, Guerrero, killing six people, wounding dozens, and forcibly disappearing 43 students. Those students are still being disappeared as I write these words. The present tense here is important, for reasons I discuss in *I Couldn't Even Imagine That They Would Kill Us: An Oral History of the Attacks Against the Students of Ayotzinapa*, published under a different title in Spanish in April 2016 and in English in November 2017.

As I worked on this book in 2013, I never even imagined that on September 26, 2014, the State would forcibly disappear 43 socially committed and combative college students approximately 57 miles away from where undercover military agents disappeared Tzompaxtle on October 25, 1996.

This books screams, or tries to. I have sought to share this with you. It should not be pleasurable. The screams are all around us and within us, and not listening to them makes it too easy to acquiesce, to accept a thinly veiled participation in the machinery that produces the screams of horror. This book aspires to combat such acquiescence, to fight against that machinery and those who operate and benefit from it. And because the screams are not only those of horror and pain, but also those of uprising—confrontation, survival, and struggle.

The structure of this book may seem frustrating to some. I try to share, in a way, the investigator's task with the reader. I show you things, share with you things I've found, but do not alert you to what I believe to be mistakes in different people's memories or reporting, or not, even though I am continually trying to show several things that I believe. But I do not tell you what is true in this story beyond that I believe in the truth of Tzompaxtle's story, and am sharing with you the reasons why. I share here what various people—several journalists, a lawyer, a social worker, a guerrilla, a brother, a partner—told me, what newspapers printed at the time, and most important, what Tzompaxtle himself told me.

This book is also concerned with the combat that different kinds of truths must face, particularly the ways in which states and courts and lawyers and laws will try to undermine the truths and the truth-telling of people who have suffered—often at the hands of the State, or in a way sanctioned by the State—by seeking out and attacking "errors" in their testimonies. One ambition of this book, in both content and form, is to disarm such strategies of delegitimization and re-victimization by showing how discrete mistakes in memory do not challenge or undermine the truth of traumatic memories, and what is more, often the "mistakes" of memory reveal truths of a different order.

THE JOURNALISTS

A MAN WALKED UNWORRIED DOWN the street. He wore
his hair and beard long and unkempt. He was on his way
to the park for a bit of exercise, to run and stretch his muscles. A well-known journalist in Chilpancingo, the capital
of Guerrero, his home state, and a man of the Left who
often wore T-shirts with images of Vladimir Lenin and
Ho Chi Minh, whose friends called him "The Wolf" or
"The Fierce Wolf" or "Steppenwolf." From 1974 to 1981
he worked in Mexico City as a subway train conductor, and
there people called him "Locoman." When he received his
first paycheck, at the age of 18, he gave half to his parents and spent the rest taking his friends record shopping.
"Pick out any one you like," he told them. With his second
paycheck he bought a stereo. He and some friends helped
distribute *Madera*, the clandestine newspaper of the Com-
munist League of September 23, an urban guerrilla group,
in the subway. He worked his way through the Carlos
Septién García Journalism School, paying tuition with his
salary from the subway. After graduation he returned to
Chilpancingo and founded the Autonomous University of
Guerrero's radio station, Radio UAG. He wrote for various local newspapers, served as the local correspondent of

Agence France-Presse, and led the morning news program on Radio UAG.

It was around 10:00 a.m., the morning news program was over, and his plan was to go for a quick run, return home, take a shower, and hit the streets—as he did every day—to follow the news. He was strolling along when a man touched his back and said: "Hello."

He saw a face he did not recognize. "Hello," he responded.

The man wore a wig and a fake mustache.

"There's no need to be afraid," this man said, sensing the tension in the Wolf's shoulders and seeing the surprise in his face.

"I'm thinking the same thing," the Wolf said, "Look at you, you're wearing a disguise, your mustache is fake."

"No," the man said, "don't be afraid, there's no need to worry. We're not doing anything wrong."

"Okay, then. How do you know me?"

"You are Sergio Ocampo."

"Yes."

"You work in Radio UAG."

"Yes, that's right."

"Would you be interested in participating in a press conference?"

"Yeah, of course."

"We would like to invite some journalists here in Chilpancingo, in Guerrero, and maybe one or two national or international correspondents to participate in an interview."

"Ah. Okay, absolutely."

This conversation took place on an October day in 1996. Four months earlier, a previously unknown Guerrero-based guerrilla group, the Popular Revolutionary Army (EPR), had made a public appearance to coincide with the first anniversary of a police killing of local activist farmers and *campesinos*—the Aguas Blancas massacre. The EPR's move was the first time since Lucio Cabañas's guerrilla organizing from the late 1960s to the mid-1970s that an armed insurgent group had carried out a public action of such magnitude in Guerrero. It was also the first guerrilla action in Mexico since the January 1, 1994, armed uprising of the Zapatista Army of National Liberation (EZLN).

On June 28, 1995, then-governor of Guerrero state Rubén Figueroa Alcocer and his lieutenant governor, José Rubén Robles Catalán, organized the ambush of more than 90 unarmed *campesinos* traveling in two flatbed trucks between Tepetixtla and Coyuca de Benítez. The *campesinos*, members of the Campesino Organization of the Southern Sierra (OCSS), were on their way to a widely publicized protest in Atoyac. State police stopped the two trucks and opened fire on the second truck, killing 17 people and wounding 23.[1] The police filmed the massacre. They also planted guns in the murdered men's hands and then filmed and photographed them lying there on the ground. State government officials edited the video to make the massacre look like the *campesinos* had been armed and had initiated a confrontation with the police. The state government sent the manipulated images to the media. Not long afterward, however, someone leaked to journalist Ricardo Rocha the original, unedited video showing the unarmed dead. Rocha broadcast the unedited video on his nightly national news program. The case became a national and international scandal that went all the way to the Mexican Supreme Court. Figueroa resigned. None of those responsible for ordering, planning, and executing the massacre were held responsible.[2]

During the public event marking the first anniversary of the massacre, about 100 armed women and men marched out from the mountainside wearing makeshift uniforms, their faces covered with bandannas. A group of EPR combatants climbed onto the stage and read a manifesto: "We no longer wish to wait defenseless for the forces of repression and death to seize our lives with impunity."[3] The politicians present at the anniversary, including Cuauhtémoc Cárdenas—the former presidential candidate, Mexico City mayor, and co-founder of the Party of the Democratic Revolution (PRD)—left the event, scandalized. Cárdenas said that those armed men and women were "a pantomime," not a guerrilla army. The public, however, once they had recovered from the scare, applauded the armed men and women. A number of the attendees wanted to follow the guerrillas back to the mountains as they left, something the rebels did not allow. The supportive popular reaction was not surprising. In his book on armed movements, *Guerrillas: Journeys in the Insurgent World*, Jon Lee Anderson writes:

> If the conditions are right, guerrillas can emerge from within any society. If people perceive themselves to be irrevocably disenfranchised by their governments, or oppressed within their country, then violence is almost bound to occur. People take

up arms for many different reasons, ranging from outrage over economic inequities and social injustices to systematic forms of cultural, racial, and political discrimination.[4]

In Guerrero's indigenous and *campesino* communities, such reasons are among the few things to be found in abundance.

The people of Guerrero have suffered political and economic violence for decades, if not centuries. Consider the following: in 1996 the state population was about 3 million people. Two million of them had never seen a doctor. About a million of them had never set foot in an elementary school. Half of all parents did not know how to read or write. Approximately 1 million people worked in the fields and their homes every day of the week without anyone paying them a cent. Each year, hundreds of thousands of tourists filled the luxury hotels of Acapulco during their vacations. Industrial-scale poppy and marijuana production fed both domestic and international drug markets. Three out of every four roads were made exclusively of dirt. Hunger represented a mortal risk for one out of every three children born in non-indigenous communities, and half of all children born in indigenous communities.[5] In Guerrero, to be "dying of hunger" never was, and still is not, something that one says casually before lunch.

One must also consider the fact that on December 30, 1960, a soldier shot Enrique Ramírez point-blank in Chilpancingo as Mr. Ramírez tried to hang a banner that read: DEATH TO THE BAD GOVERNMENT. At the protest that formed in response to his killing, soldiers first shoved and beat people, then opened fire on the crowd. The soldiers killed fourteen people, including three children, and wounded forty. A year later, state police killed eight people and wounded at least ten more from the Guerrero Civic Association led by Genaro Vázquez, a schoolteacher. They were protesting electoral fraud. On May 18, 1967, just as schoolteacher Lucio Cabañas grabbed the microphone to address a crowd of parents and teachers from the Juan N. Álvarez Elementary School, state police mixed in with the crowd, took positions on rooftops, and opened fire on the crowd. Five people were killed and twenty wounded. Three months later, state police massacred eighty agricultural workers in Acapulco.[6]

Lucio Cabañas escaped from what came to be known as the Atoyac Massacre and took up arms, founding the Party of the Poor in 1967. Genaro Vázquez got tired of state repression, took up arms, and founded the National Revolutionary Civic Association in 1969. Both Cabañas and Vázquez were rural elementary school teachers and graduates of the Raúl Isidro Burgos Rural Teachers College in Ayotzinapa, Guerrero. The Mexican federal government sent a third of its armed forces to kill both men, "disappearing" hundreds—some say thousands—of people in the process.[7]

"Guerrilla movements in Guerrero have been constant," writes Carlos Montemayor in his essay "*La guerrilla recurrente*" (The Recurring Guerrilla War).[8] He argues that armed movements represent "the final, armed phase of a prior social violence."[9] The state, Montemayor writes, always denies these social roots of armed movements, insisting on viewing and representing guerrilla groups as military threats to "social peace" that can only be addressed through a military campaign of annihilation. Thus successive governments send development projects and death squads to the rebel territories until they feel satisfied with the tally of the dead. Then they leave. With this experience of social trauma as both a motivating and a unifying factor, the survivors, the witnesses, and the families of the disappeared and the dead begin to organize and, some time later, once again rise up in arms. "The peace achieved through negotiation and social change would be one thing," writes Montemayor, "the peace achieved via the extermination of the social bases and insurgent core groups quite another. According to the Mexican experience, we may conclude that every time the state has opted to exterminate the social bases, they have set in place the conditions for the recurrence of guerrilla war."[10]

On August 28, 1996, two months after its first public appearance at the anniversary of the Aguas Blancas massacre, EPR commandos simultaneously attacked police and soldiers in various cities across four states. That day eight police, three soldiers, two civilians, and two guerrillas died in the attacks. More than 20 people sustained gunshot wounds.[11] The guerrillas were not pantomiming.

Sergio Ocampo wondered whether or not the guy with the fake mustache was connected with the guerrillas. "I didn't have any contacts," Ocampo told me. "I had met some people from the guerrillas when I worked in the subway. But when I came here to Chilpancingo, everything had been shattered by the repression and the disappearances of thousands of people. At that time, here at the university, there was no revolutionary energy."

During the 1980s and the early 1990s, Ocampo saw communiqués from the verbosely named Clandestine Revolutionary Workers Party—Union of the People—Party of the Poor (PROCUP-PDLP) published in newspapers like Mexico City's *La Jornada* and *Unomásuno*.[12] He had never, however, attended a clandestine press conference with the guerrillas, as none are known to have been held during those years. The man who approached him in the street asked him to invite other journalists to gather later at a restaurant. A contact would meet them there.

Ocampo invited Maribel Gutiérrez, who wrote for both *La Jornada* and *El Sur* (based at that time in Acapulco); Héctor Téllez, a photographer with *El Sur*; Jesús Guerrero, a correspondent with *Reforma*, a newspaper in Mexico City, and the German agency DPA; and a Guatemalan reporter living in Chilpancingo.[13] When the contact arrived, he gestured to the Guatemalan and said: "He can't go; he's too tall and not from here. He'll get you all in trouble." The Guatemalan reporter had to leave.

The contact gave Ocampo purple strips of paper with instructions printed in linotype. Ocampo read them and then destroyed them. He told me: "The instructions that I remember said to go to Tierra Colorada, take a bus to Acapulco. From Acapulco go to Frog Park, I think, or Turtle Park, frog or turtle. Walk through the park. Walk back. Take another bus to Chilpancingo. Go to Zumpango."

Jesús Guerrero told me that they spent two days going around in circles before getting to the final meeting point. "These kinds of meetings with the guerrillas are not easy.

You have to take all kinds of security measures. We were in Acapulco for a day and a night, and then on Friday they brought us back. We had to go to Chilpancingo after passing through Tierra Colorada and then on to Zumpango."

Maribel Gutiérrez barely recalled the initial trips they made. "That was a long time ago," she told me. "I've done fifteen hundred things since then. What is more, we had no idea that everything would become so important and would have to do with something so serious as someone getting disappeared. But, yes, we had been traveling for a day, perhaps two days."

Héctor Téllez said they had been traveling for two days. "We went through various municipalities in Guerrero state: Acapulco, Tierra Caliente, Costa Chica. We finally got to Zumpango del Río. We made contact with the guerrillas' personnel there."

The four journalists arrived at the central plaza in Zumpango del Río sometime between seven and eight at night on October 25, 1996. Ocampo recalls, "The final directions said: 'Go to the park in Zumpango, you will see a man with a black [Chicago] Bulls hat.' I remember that the Bulls symbol is a red animal, an ox or something. That was the last instruction we received. We didn't have any problems. Then we got to the park and it seemed like a hundred people were wearing baseball caps. Not all were Bulls caps, but several were. If I remember correctly, at that point in the 1990s Michael Jordan was the king of basketball. Everyone had Bulls caps.[14]

"We walked in circles around the park and started getting nervous," Ocampo told me. "We sat down for a while to watch the different people wearing Bulls caps, looking to see if any of them looked like they could be guerrillas. We didn't see anyone. About 20 minutes after getting there, two young men walked by and gestured to us with a nod of their heads. We gestured to them the same way and then followed them."

Jesús Guerrero, Héctor Téllez, and Maribel Gutiérrez did not mention this part of the story. Ocampo, in contrast, emphasized the time they spent walking around the plaza looking for the contact with a Bulls cap: "We were on the west side of the park and, after walking around in circles, when we sat down, well, sure, it was confusing; people looked at us strangely. It would have been easy for military intelligence to spot us. The EPR attacks had just happened. I remember well that those old books about the Bolshevik Revolution said to be wary of parks. Parks are not ideal for people involved in these kinds of activities."

When I asked her about that night, one of the first things that Gutiérrez told me was: "If we had known, do you think we wouldn't have written about it for the newspapers? That would have been very unprofessional of us, to say the least. In the moment, we didn't understand anything."

Ocampo returned to the moment when they established contact: "Two boys walked by nodding to us. I think they were indigenous or *campesino* and maybe 14, 15, or 16 years old. One of them was wearing a Bulls cap. We walked behind them. Out of nowhere we heard a sound like a firecracker. As soon as we heard the sound, the two *compas** started shouting: 'We've got a tail! We've got a tail!' We

---

* Short for compañero or compañera, a friend and companion in struggle.

had been walking in a line down a narrow, dark street that would take us to a dirt road. 'We've got a tail! We've got a tail!' Much later they told me that the sound we thought was a firecracker was actually a gunshot. Time to run! We all started running. I didn't see that one of the *compas* had been grabbed."

This is what Gutiérrez told me had happened: "A number of journalists from different media were on our way to an interview. And then, all of a sudden, they told us that . . . I don't remember exactly, it was a long time ago: 'We're being followed. You all need to go; the interview is suspended. Everything is cancelled. Keep going along this path, you'll arrive over there, alone.' And that's what we did. We didn't know anything else. I don't remember how much time passed after that night when they grabbed him—but it was much later—that we learned that he had been going with us."

This is what Guerrero told me had happened: "We got there around seven or eight at night. We were in this little plaza where we were to meet the contact. After a while, we saw a group of militants coming our way with their backpacks, maybe about four or six of them. They were marching. I thought it was strange. We got to the plaza. It is a small town and people easily recognize who's who. What's up with a group like this, marching? I thought: 'If the cops see these guys they'll shoot 'em dead right here.'

"Then they took us out to this hill," Guerrero continued. "Walking away from the plaza, away from town, uphill, I think heading toward the highway, they handed us some water containers. We kept walking. We went by a trash dump.

"The guy next to me was Rafael. He said: 'We've got a tail, we've got a tail." And we all started running. I knew it was him because I saw his face and recognized it. We came to a kind of ravine and hid there. After a while we went farther, toward a barbed-wire fence. I heard something like when someone chambers a bullet in a gun. I guessed it was the *compas*. Then they shouted out to someone. One of the *compas* grabbed Maribel and lifted her over the fence. We climbed over the fence. They took us to a kind of ravine. Sergio says—I didn't see it—that some of the *compas* had taken out their guns, in case soldiers or military intelligence showed up.

"Someone said: 'It's not going to happen; we're suspending the interview.' They left then. We stayed there hiding for about 20 minutes. Then we started out again and came upon a high school near a hill and saw a bonfire. There were some students partying there. We also saw a white van. My guess was that the van belonged to the Army, the men who grabbed Rafael."

This is what Téllez told me had happened: "They took us away from the zócalo in Zumpango del Río. We were on the edge of the town when we heard a gunshot. One of the guides said that the interview would be cancelled because they were being watched. At that moment we heard that one of the members of their group had been grabbed—the one who had been taking care of the security of the journalists—and the leaders told us that the press conference had to be cancelled. So we left. We took a different route near a dry riverbed and got to the highway. Disappointed, we then went to Chilpancingo. You know, before getting to Zumpango del Río we had spent two days wandering through different municipalities until they felt safe, but . . . their security protocols failed when their compañero got taken."

Ocampo continued describing what happened like this: "We all ran toward a cliff. I'd say we ran about 300 meters. We ran quite a bit until one of those boys who was acting as the rearguard helped us get over a fence. I remember that he grabbed Maribel and picked her up and set her down on the other side of a barbed-wire fence. He took an AK-47 out of his backpack. He told us: 'Go!' And we said: 'You go on. We doubt they'll do anything to us.' So the boy took off. Then we came out near a high school building, I think it is the UAG High School 36 that is there in Zumpango. We saw all sorts of strange things on that walk. We were already, you could say, freaked out by everything that had happened. We took a mini-bus back to Chilpancingo."

All the journalists except Téllez told me that they did not know that someone had been taken that night until the EPR published its first communiqué. Téllez, in contrast, said that they did know then, but he did not mention any of the EPR communiqués denouncing the forced disappearance.

Ocampo told me: "Later, three days later, the newspapers published the communiqué, saying that one of those guys we met that night had been detained. Later we found out that his name was Rafael. I felt really bad. I thought: 'What mistake did I make?' We didn't have cell phones then, and they prohibited us from using the phone at all. Did one of the other reporters use the phone? What happened?"

Guerrero said: "A week or so later, I can't remember exactly, the EPR sent a communiqué saying that one of the *compas* had been disappeared. Didn't he escape later? Didn't he return to civilian life?"

Gutiérrez said: "We didn't know anything that night, not until a long time later when the bulletin came out. But we weren't even sure about that, or anything."

Téllez said: "None of it caused a stir until the state government found a safe house in Palomares, Acapulco, where the so-called Rafael had lived. They found uniforms, bandannas, and letters to the editors of *El Sol de Acapulco*, *El Sur*, *Novedades*, *Diario 17*. . . . "

Everyone except Téllez speculated as to what may have happened. Gutiérrez said: "Look, did they grab Rafael because of us? I don't think so. Or because we made a mistake with the directions or followed the wrong person? No. No."

Guerrero said: "I feel like what happened that day in Zumpango was the guerrillas' mistake. Why did they send us to such a visible place? . . . There was a clash between guerrillas and police near Zumpango. Near the Curva del Cristo there was an ambush. On June 28, 1996, when the EPR made a public appearance in Aguas Blancas, they also carried out several other actions, including one in the Curva del Cristo. They ambushed a group of police and wounded one or two of them. With the appearance of that EPR cell, the state sent a shit ton of spies to Zumpango. I think that it was a mistake having us go there. There were eyes all over that place."

Throughout my interview with him, Ocampo continually came back to the issue of responsibility: "We don't know whether the state had already seen us traveling through so many places: Chilpancingo, Tierra Colorada, and Acapulco, back and forth again. I later thought that it would have been easy to have us meet them somewhere along a highway or something, and if they'd seen that we were being followed they could have sent us a message, or just left us standing there. We already knew that we were supposed to wait ten minutes and if no one came, then they wouldn't be coming. . . . We were left wondering what had happened. That was really hard because later we learned how they tortured that guy. Everyone . . . I at least felt a weight on my conscience, because they tortured him really badly. . . . I think, I don't know . . . I can't tell you that we didn't make some mistake. Maybe we did. But we followed their instructions to a T."

THE NEWS REPORTS

ON NOVEMBER 4, 1996, THE newspaper *El Sol de Aca-pulco* published the following on its front page, above the masthead: "One of our militants held prisoner and incommunicado since ten days ago: EPR." The front-page article, signed by Javier Trujillo Juárez, appeared above the fold with the headline: "Rafael, the first prisoner to be recognized by the masked ones," and the subheading: "They demand he be presented alive." The article states the following:

> Rafael is the first prisoner of war of the self-proclaimed Popular Revolutionary Army (EPR). He was captured and kidnapped by members of the Mexican Army who were disguised as civilians.
>
> The insurgent group's regional military General Command released the above information in an EPR communiqué dated last November first and signed by Commandant "Antonio."
>
> In the document, the armed group demands that the combatant Rafael—his nom de guerre—be immediately presented before the authorities. The document states that Rafael was captured in front

of various eyewitnesses near Zumpango del Río on Friday, October 25.

The next six paragraphs give a summary of the EPR's communiqué. A second section of the same article describes "a new EPR attack" against "a police outpost in Teloloapan; no casualties were reported on either side."

That same day, November 4, 1996, *La Jornada* published a four-paragraph article by Maribel Gutiérrez on page 16 with the headline: "EPR: A militant was captured during the ceasefire," and the subheading: "He has not been taken to authorities nor seen by the press: Antonio." The article provides a brief summary of the group's communiqué and closes with this quotation from it:

> The detention and kidnapping of this combatant occurred before the expiration of the unilateral truce (October 27 at 20:30 hours) that our army declared once the government made public declarations calling for supposed talks, while that same government represses, disappears, and tortures.

On November 6, 1996, *El Sol de Acapulco* published an article by Chilpancingo correspondent José Manuel Benítez on the upper right-hand side of the front page with the headline: "The governor knew about the detention of Rafael from the EPR." The article says:

> Governor Ángel Aguirre Rivero said that he knew about the detention of Rafael, a member of the so-called Popular Revolutionary Army (EPR), stating

that he would no longer offer to hold talks [with the group], since they do not desire such talks.

Interviewed at the end of a ceremony for the signing of the Alliance for Economic Growth in the state, the governor was asked if he knew about the detention in Zumpango del Río last October 25 of a member of the EPR, as charged in the armed group's communiqué.

The governor answered: "Yes I know about it; of course, I'm aware as state governor, but it is not my job to be giving information about the details. I wouldn't know what to tell you all."

The five-paragraph article continues on page five, where the governor says that he will not make another offer to hold talks since the EPR has rejected such offers with its ongoing acts of aggression against police and soldiers. The reporter then cites the governor as stating that in his meeting with the federal Secretary of Gobernación (the most powerful member of the Mexican Cabinet) they did not talk about the armed group, and then confirmed that the federal budget for Guerrero state would triple in the coming year, "to address important items such as health, education, public safety, and others."

On November 11, 1996, *El Sol de Acapulco* published an article by José Manuel Benítez on the upper right-hand corner of the front page with the headline: "The Army still has not handed him over to the state PGR" (Attorney General). The article accompanies a blurry, black-and-white photograph of a face with a one-word caption: "Rafael."

The piece opens with this sentence:

> The Army still has not taken the supposed member
> of the self-proclaimed Popular Revolutionary Army
> (EPR), called Rafael, to the Federal Attorney General,
> said the state PGR delegate, Agustín Peniche
> Álvarez.

The article's second paragraph mentions the EPR
communiqué sent a week before. Then it states:

> The PGR delegate did not comment on whether
> or not the Mexican Army had informed them about
> the detention of the presumed EPRista, as denounced
> by the armed group, but if such were true,
> he said: "they still have not delivered him to us so
> that we may proceed as need be."

The remaining five paragraphs describe the PGR's efforts
to investigate and arrest members of the armed group.

On November 12, 1996, *La Jornada* published an article
by Maribel Gutiérrez on page 14 with the headline:
"Denial of reports of captured EPR militant." The article's
opening paragraphs read:

> General Edmundo Elpidio Leyva Galindo, commandant
> of the Ninth Military Region based in
> Acapulco, refused yesterday to provide information
> about the capture and disappearance of a member of
> the Popular Revolutionary Army (EPR) by soldiers

last October 25 in Zumpango. Meanwhile, in two communiqués the EPR demanded that authorities demonstrate that "the combatant Rafael" is alive and that his status as "prisoner of war" be respected.

When asked in Acapulco, General Leyva Galindo maintained that he was not authorized "to make that kind of a comment." However, he did not deny the events revealed by the EPR and told reporters that only the National Defense Secretariat could provide the relevant information.

The remaining seven paragraphs quote the general denying "categorically that Guerrero is militarized," and then provide a brief summary of two EPR communiqués released the day before demanding that the military prove that the man they disappeared is still alive and that they hand him over to the proper civilian authorities.

On November 18, 1996, *El Sur* published a four-paragraph article on page three with the headline: "'No comment' about Rafael's capture." The article, which does not include a byline, quotes General Edmundo Elpido Leyva Galindo, commandant of the Ninth Military Region. Asked about the EPR's communiqués denouncing combatant Rafael's disappearance, General Galindo replies: "I am not authorized to make that kind of comment." Asked about the Army's presence in Guerrero after the EPR's public appearance, the general responds:

There has definitely not been an increase. What's happening is that we are moving around more trying to cover more territory, but Guerrero is not being militarized. Over time there has always been this presence; in the regions where we are located, as in the mountains, people view us as friends.

On December 4, 1996, *El Sol de Acapulco* published an article by Javier Soriana Guerrero on page five with the headline: "New EPR communiqué again denounces Rafael's disappearance." The opening paragraphs read:

"In the face of the Mexican people's just struggles for work, justice, democracy, and liberty, the government has responded with all the State's might," states a communiqué from the Democratic Revolutionary Party and the General Command of the Popular Revolutionary Army sent to this newspaper yesterday.

Last night during an anonymous call, a man's voice said that an EPR communiqué addressed to *El Sol de Acapulco* could be found next to a corner store on Capitán Malaspina Street.

The EPRistas' document is addressed to the armed forces, and points out that the Army defends the interests of the 24 multimillionaires who dominate Mexico, trampling the Mexican people's rights, and ignoring the pain and lives of those who proclaim their discontent concerning the current state of affairs.

They call out to the "Mexican Soldier," indicating that the Homeland does not mean the 24 oligarchs, but the 93 million Mexicans, 65 million of whom are to be found in poverty and whose situation gets worse by the day, and saying, "Amongst those poor you'll find your family . . . you'll find yourself."

The remaining six paragraphs continue to summarize the communiqué and only mention Rafael's case in the penultimate paragraph, when the reporter paraphrases the EPR: "Having honor means refusing to torture or to murder innocent people, or children, as happened recently in Chilpancingo, Guerrero; to refuse the Dirty War* to detain, torture, and disappear prisoners of war, like Rafael, an EPR combatant in Guerrero."

On December 8, 1996, *El Sol de Acapulco* published an article signed by Javier Trujillo Juárez on the lower left-hand part of the front page, with the following two headlines: "EPR calls out to NGO," and "Asks them to intercede with the government to present Rafael." The article continues on page nine and consists of nine paragraphs that summarize the EPR communiqué dated December 6, 1996.

On December 9, 1996, *El Sur* published an article that filled almost all of page five, with the headline: "Don't give

---

*   The term "Dirty War" used in the EPR communiqués and press reports refers to the practices of State terrorism—namely the systematic use of torture, murder, and forced disappearance of members of armed insurgencies, suspected members of or sympathizers with armed insurgencies, people involved in unarmed social struggle, people living in regions with active or suspected insurgencies, or people simply labeled enemies of the State—carried out in Mexico roughly between the late 1960s and the mid-1980s, though—as Tzompaxtle's torture and disappearance show—the practices were never discontinued.

up, endure the torture, a message from the EPR to Rafael in a video." The article, by Misael Habana de los Santos, describes a video recording sent by the armed group to *El Sur*:

> The video lasts eight minutes and was accompanied by a photograph of the guerrilla detained by plain-clothes members of the Mexican Army, taken to Military Zone 35 in Chilpancingo, and, according to accounts obtained by this reporter, later taken to the base of the Ninth Region in Cumbres de Llano Largo in Acapulco, from where he was finally sent to the Military Base Number One.

A package left outside the newspaper's office in Acapulco contained a VHS cassette, a color photograph of the combatant Rafael, and two communiqués. One communiqué was addressed to human rights organizations, and the other was a "list of events related to the combatant Rafael's detention." The article provides a brief summary of the "list of events" and then offers "the non-official version of the events":

> According to state police sources, Rafael confessed his links to the armed group that appeared in Aguas Blancas last June 28 to a compadre and, according to the same source, had invited him to participate. His compadre told his boss about the identity of the EPR combatant and his boss, in turn, personally told the leader of the Military Zone 35, Efraín Leyva García, who organized the operation against

Rafael, whom he had been following from the moment of the betrayal up until Rafael's capture in Zumpango del Río.

According to the same source, Rafael was taken to Military Zone 35, where he was interrogated for the first time. Later he was taken by helicopter to the base of the Ninth Military Region in Cumbres de Llano Largo, in Acapulco, still under the leadership of the commandant Edmundo Elpidio Leyva Galindo, whereupon he was taken to the Military Camp Number One in Mexico City, where he is supposedly being held.

The remaining five paragraphs describe an eight-minute video featuring a woman wearing a gray bandanna and a thick tan shirt. With the sound of the Andean group Los Calchakis playing in the background and a white sheet hung as a backdrop, the woman looks directly into the camera and identifies herself as Rafael's wife. The video edits together three segments, each shot from a different position. Misael Habana de los Santos writes:

The woman interrupts her testimony multiple times; at times her voice breaks with the pain of losing her husband Rafael, other times, due to the nervousness the camera causes her and "because of the risk I am taking." There is drama, especially when she shows Rafael's photo, and when her small daughter seeks her out, and comes up to her with only her head showing in the video. When the

woman speaks of her children she says "nosotras"
[the feminine plural of "us"].

The reporter then quotes directly from the woman's
testimony, parenthetically inserting his own descriptions:

To The People, to everyone who sees me and hears
me. I want to tell you that I am the wife of Rafael
who was detained on October 25 in Zumpango del
Río. They have not presented him before authorities, and like him, many other people have also been
disappeared. Now that they have kidnapped him I
have learned that he was a member of that organization, but at the time I did not know that my
husband participated. I do not plan on giving up my
demand for him.

Rafael, wherever you are, wherever they have
you, if you are alive, I want to tell you that the children are well (she cries and pauses) we miss you so
much (the children's cries can be heard). I wish this
hadn't happened (she raises her hand to her head,
wearing a long-sleeved shirt), but this is the reality.
The only thing I can tell you is not to surrender. If
they are torturing you, endure all the torture because that would help us a lot, you would help your
family and especially the organization. . . . Don't
give up!

If you come back alive someday you will find
us here. We are not alone because we remain united. We have our family. You are also not alone.
The Popular Revolutionary Army supports you.

(Weeping, she raises her hand to her eyes. Long pause during which only the music can be heard.) You have to be very strong. You always told me that I should take care of the children. I will take care of them, and I know that you will return. I will wait for you always. (The shadow of someone giving her something can be seen. As a child approaches her, she then lifts a photograph of Rafael. She and the child both cry.)

I know that it is a risk to be here, but this is a decision that I have made, and I will continue to demand that they account for you and prove that you are alive. If you see us or hear us someday, we love you, the children and me.

On December 18, 1996, *El Sol de Acapulco* published a front-page, four-column headline: "Rafael's Car Found." Beneath the headline is a photograph showing two men in a white Volkswagen Beetle leaving a parking lot through a wide exit toward the street. The photo caption reads: "Authorities confiscated yesterday the car that the EPRista Rafael left in a public parking lot in Chilpancingo." On the upper left-hand portion of the front page, the corresponding article, written by Rodrigo Carmona Casiano, begins with the headline: "The EPRista left it in a parking lot in Chilpo."

The article leads with this sentence:

Yesterday afternoon the State Investigative Police (PJE) removed a white Volkswagen with the license plate number GZF-9281 from the public parking lot known as Vélez; the car was left there by Rafael, the combatant of the Popular Revolutionary Army (EPR), on Friday October 25 of this year.

The reporter quotes the officer in charge of the forfeiture and then writes:

> At one point, one of the managers of the parking lot, who asked to remain anonymous, said that during the past 52 days the car had been under surveillance by military intelligence officers. "They prohibited us from saying anything to the media."
> He maintained that on October 28 (two days after combatant Rafael's capture) military intelligence officers arrived at the parking lot and searched the car. "They took some documents, like guerrilla propaganda, and from that moment they began a strict surveillance of the area surrounding the lot."
> He mentioned that the car was in fact left there on the morning of Friday, October 25, which coincides with the list of events published a few days before by the armed group, which had indicated that after leaving the car there, the rebel then went to Zumpango, where he was captured by military intelligence officers at nine in the morning.

On February 5, 1997, *El Sol de Acapulco* published a front-page, four-column headline: "Discovery of guerrilla materials." The accompanying photograph shows a number of men armed with machine and submachine guns guarding the white door of a house. A man in civilian clothes covers his face with one hand, apparently a gesture for the photographers to step back. The article by Celso Castro Castro and Javier Trujillo Juárez features the subheading: "Presumably it belongs to the EPR: explosives, uniforms and propaganda found."

The opening paragraphs read:

> In a joint raid of a private residence yesterday, agents from the Federal Attorney General (PGR) and the State Investigative Police (PJE) secured homemade explosive devices, uniforms, and subversive material, presumably belonging to the armed group known as the Popular Revolutionary Army (EPR). No one was arrested.
>
> The commanding officers of the two police forces contradicted each other. Initially the director of the PJE, Francisco Vargas Nájera, informed that officers went to the private residence located at 227 Vicente Guerrero Street inside the "Adolfo López Mateos" apartment complex (better know as Los Palomares) after receiving an anonymous call from a teenager at 13:00 hours, and that said teenager notified the police of the discovery.
>
> Vargas Nájera immediately notified the general supervisor, Tomás Herrera Basurto, who, leading two groups, went to the location indicated by the anonymous source and verified that the residence in question consisted of concrete and asbestos sheets, two garages, and a bedroom where police found uniforms, combat boots, subversive printed materials, and more than a dozen homemade explosive devices.

He said that upon realizing this fell under federal jurisdiction, he informed the office of the Federal Attorney General (PGR). He also notified the office that he had taken necessary steps to secure the building in case it was wired with explosives.

The article continues on page two. The reporters describe the arrival of the Guerrero state delegate and sub-delegate of the Federal Attorney General, who refused to provide information and ordered the police to keep anyone from getting near the residence. The article continues:

> At 8:30 p.m., Rebeca Sereiz Robles, the owner of the property, arrived and was immediately interrogated by Federal Investigative Police agents; she notified them that the residence had been rented by some people who had not paid the rent and for that reason she had gone to see them yesterday, meeting with the unpleasant surprise that her property had been used for other purposes. She then immediately notified the authorities through a relative.

According to authorities, that's when the police entered the building. Soon afterward, officials outside the residence told the members of the press that they had found the following:

> More than a dozen pairs of boots, uniforms, gray bulletproof vests, 7.62 caliber cartridges (used for AK-47 assault rifles), various manuals with different names, gunpowder, a bag of combined fertilizers,

bags of sawdust, guerrilla military instruction books, wooden rifle stocks for AK-47s.

Additionally, masking tape, a book of matches, prepared fertilizers, cigarette lighters, sodium chloride and sugar, homemade climont mines (sic), bags of armonal, electronic activating devices, homemade explosives using car exhaust pipes, slingshots for activating bombs, bomb devices, a Smith & Wesson 9 millimeter pistol, watch batteries, a gun clip, a large pair of pliers, telephone wire, circuitry wires, lamp bulbs, clothespins, soldering irons, welding pastes, hemp thread, iron, fishing line, tweezers, scissors, a box cutter, plastic cables, and a mechanic's toolbox.

The next day *El Sol de Acapulco* published an article by Javier Trujillo Juárez with the headline: "Police secure artifacts and propaganda from presumed EPR house." The subheading reads: "It had been abandoned since October." The piece appears on the left-hand aide of the front page beneath the fold. The article reports that the objects found in the residence, "including a guitar," were removed from the building under "heavy police guard." In the article's fifth paragraph the writer reports:

Minutes later two military officers arrived, a lieutenant colonel and a colonel; they both entered the house accompanied by immediate response personnel from the National Secretariat of Gobernación (SEGOB). No further information concerning the military officers was provided.

The reporter mentions again that police found explosive materials of an unknown type in the house and then writes:

> A neighbor who asked that her name not be published said that for more than a year the house had been occupied by "a family that looked like campesinos that had three cars: a Ram pickup and two white Volkswagen Beetles. They were also a bit strange, because they would enter and leave either really early or really late, almost at dawn, and they didn't socialize with anyone.
>
> The neighbor maintained that "the man that lived there was with his wife, a woman, and they lived there with two children. The woman even gave birth to one of them here, but since October they had abandoned the place."

On February 10, 1997, *El Sur* published a four-paragraph article without a byline. The piece appeared in the corner of page six with the headline: "Now I wouldn't call the EPR to talks: Aguirre." The article reports that during a press conference, Governor Ángel Aguirre Rivero rejected the possibility of establishing talks with the EPR. Afterward, in the last paragraph, the article states:

> Then, regarding the fact that the armed group had written in one if its communiqués that the governor had acknowledged the detention of its combatant, in contrast to the Army which denies any participation

in the capture, Aguirre said: "I never said that I acknowledged that that person was apprehended; I said that I had learned about the supposed detention of the combatant Rafael in the press."

THEY TEAR YOU FROM THE WORLD

IT IS NINE O'CLOCK AT night. Two men stop about five meters in front of you. They start to fight. Another man walks up to them. You and your compañero approach them, wary, to pass them. The third man pulls out a pistol and jumps you. You grab his hand and the barrel of the pistol trying to take the gun. The two of you struggle. Your compañero dodges the other two men and runs. You hear a gunshot and then, in an instant, the other two men take you to the ground. The three of them pin you. They speak into a portable two-way radio. They take off your belt and use it to tie your hands behind you. They blindfold you.

All of this happens in a matter of seconds.*

---

* The narrative in the chapters *They Tear You from the World* and *A Piece of Being* is built upon more than thirty hours of recorded interviews I conducted with Andrés Tzompaxtle Tecpile and a written testimony dated "Spring 1999" that Tzompaxtle gave me. All the italicized words are direct quotes from the interviews with Tzompaxtle: They are his words. All non-italicized dialogue and quoted text without footnotes are taken from Tzompaxtle's written testimony: They are also his words. The sources for all other quotations may be found in the endnotes. All non-cited text is my writing.

Your eyes: blindfolded. Your hands: bound. You think: *now it's my turn.* You ask yourself if you will be able to endure it, if you will be able to resist, if you will die. You think of your compañera and the *treasure* she holds in her arms. And you tell them goodbye.

The first beatings and questions come in the vehicle. Who are you? Are you from the EPR? Who were the others? Where are they going now? Where was the next meeting point? Where? They stop and take you out of the vehicle. You think you must be on the outskirts of Chilpancingo. You can hear the sounds of the highway in the distance. You don't know this yet, but *these first minutes are important for them.*

They remove your clothes and *wrap you in blankets. They put you on the rack and tie you down with cords and strips of cloth, completely immobilizing you. They leave only your toes and your head uncovered so they can connect the electrical wires there and close the circuit. You are completely wet. They bind your head down against the rack with strips of cloth, immobilizing it. The defense instincts of the body are mutilated.*

They beat you without rest using their fists and the stocks of their pistols. There are about eight or ten people beating you now. More of them are giving orders, watching, or waiting their turn. You can't see anyone, or anything. You don't know when the blows will hit or where they will hit. The strikes impact as if materializing from nothing. You cannot move. One man stuffs a wet rag into your mouth. Another shoots water up your nose. They pour water all over your wrapped body. And then they begin with the electric shocks, first to your feet.

This is not some street fight where you can see your

opponent, and that has a serious impact. You cannot see them. You do not know where the blows "will rain down," as they would say. You don't know where they'll hit you: on the mouth, the nose, the genitals, or the hands . . . If you could open your eyes, maybe you wouldn't even be afraid of being beaten because you'd be looking at your aggressor. Not here: You are reduced to a bulk, an object that can be beaten at their will. This has a psychological impact. For you darkness is the only thing real. This reduces you to something even more broken. There is no more . . . you can't defend yourself.[1]

They work on your body with precision and efficiency. They have come prepared. But you haven't. A few minutes ago, for example, you had never felt *like your brain is exploding. You did not know that the pain concentrates in the brain. The torture instruments of antiquity really have nothing on these men. They are so precise; they know how to directly reach the brain and burn it.*

And the issue is that *these first minutes are important for them.*

What can you see? Nothing. Is there any light? You don't know. Sound is all there is: their demented shouts and, in the background, some loud, monotonous music, a hissing that assaults your ears. It's as if they had torn you from the world and put you in some other place where you lie bound and lacking. You are a vulnerable being without sight, without feet, without hands. You are not the adult they just grabbed, but a person who, just from this change of worlds, has been utterly mutilated. You have no form. This is a state of mutilation, and has been from the beginning.

In only a few minutes, your body feels more pain than many people will experience in a lifetime. And you can't scream. Your body contracts, your bones contract, and at any moment everything will explode. Pain and fear. How long will this last? Will you endure? Will they kill you? There is no way to know. *They take you to a reality that is not the one you know.* The risk is immense and it constricts you and it is not only that you may die, but that *they can reduce you; they can change you. They remove the gag from your mouth so you can surrender. They tell you: "Help yourself!"* But, what is this "help"? It is betrayal.

If they can conquer you in the first minutes then they will have an advantage. If you don't adjust to this world, if you don't retain your conscience, if you don't resist it, they can, in a matter of minutes, change you completely. They have their objective; they have experience; they have been schooled and they have done this for many years.

How long have you been here now? *Your notion of time no longer applies.* A doctor approaches and checks your vital signs. He says you can take some more *but they should let you breathe.* You can hear a boss criticizing his minions: that they shouldn't pour water down your mouth and nose at the same time as they connect the cables because that could kill you too quickly. The boss screams: *"Break him! Increase the voltage! Break him into pieces!" This is not to make you afraid: This is to destroy you.*

They have medical services here, but not for the right to health: There are no rights here, not even *the right to die.* There are water and electricity. You feel like life is flowing out of you, but then you return to pain, to the beatings, that is, to your skin and flesh tearing, to the blood spilling from your mouth and nose.

In a place like this, one views life through a different

optic. Someone might say: "It is just an issue of taking it, that's what you've got to do."

No. You don't know if you'll make it. That depends on them, they might even kill you by accident. Many people do not come back from this. Thousands have not come back. This is the force of the State. They themselves say so and brag: "This is the face and the true force of the State." Yes, without a doubt it is.

And again the questions: What is your name? What is your *nom de guerre*? Where are you from? What military action were you going to carry out? Where? Who is your contact?

You don't respond. You know that the questions mean pain and death. If you answer, the information will be used to locate your compañeros and your family and torture them, disappear them, or kill them. If you do not answer, then they will torture you more and the moment of your disappearance or death will inch closer. You cannot think it over. You cannot calculate or reflect. They ask. You don't answer by instinct. The blows rain down. Your body contracts and explodes at the same time. Your nose, broken. Where is your safe house? They remove the gag. Your silence. The electric shocks and the pain.

No word can tell this. No sentence, no story, no metaphor expresses this pain. Pain breaks the words, the language. "Intense pain is world-destroying. Intense pain is also language-destroying: As the content of one's world disintegrates, so the content of one's language disintegrates."[2] The scream remains, though cut down by the wet rag in your mouth, and your throat cracks dry with your futile effort to expel the pain. Your entire naked body is wet and in pain, but thirst begins to rip at you from inside.

There is no part of your body that is not under attack. But this is only beginning. You are still livid. *It is not so easy to reduce you*. The pain increases at thirty minutes per second. You want with all your being for them to untie you just for a moment, just for a bit. You think: *Okay, if you're looking for a fight, you've got it, let's do it, but with a bit more honor*. You tell them to let you up for a second. Sure, they say, and they keep at it. The electric shocks. And they beat you along your spine. *No. There is no honor here. They do not know what honor is*. The doctor says: *Bend his hands back; punish his genitals*.

Now they make you feel the closest signs of death. What it feels like to die. They are showing that to you now. This brings forth a different kind of fear. You think: *Yes, I'm pretty tough, but I don't want to die*. Do they threaten to kill you? *No. They are not threatening you; they are telling you. This is their work. They don't want to scare you*.

Again the questions: What is your name? And you speak. But you remain on guard. You speak to get a respite. You give them a false name. And they beat you. And you go on. The respite is infinitesimal and you need and long for another. Questions and answers. Here, with your body tied to the rack. "The question, whatever its content, is an act of wounding; the answer, whatever its content, is a scream."[3] Are you one of them? *Yes, yes I'm one of them*. Who is your contact? You don't answer. They box your ears. Strangle you. They hit your head, your muscles. They tell you they are going to castrate you, they are going to rape you with an Iguana's tail. Water and the electric shocks. *They take you to the true scene of pain. They make you live the maximum human pain, the height, the threshold. And this threshold is the thread that divides life and death*.

Death also seduces you.[4] You fear it and want to avoid it. But there are moments when, in order not to surrender to them and not to have to endure any more, you want to give yourself to death. *There are moments when the anguish is so terrible that you'd rather die, in fact death becomes the refuge, the hope. The pain is so . . . so indescribable, so unbearable, that it's better to die. And death is not your desire, but in this moment death signifies refuge, the sensation of rest. That's why you look for it, you seek it, not because you really want to die, but because this other reality is worse.*

But no. They are not going to kill you yet. That's why the doctor is here. They want to take care of your life so they can better administer your death. They don't want you to rest: they want you to come apart. They want you to break. *You are the experiment.* You are the first guerrilla fighter captured in Guerrero state since the massive Army operation that killed Lucio Cabañas in 1974. *The first.*

When they say that you're the first, they are being honest and clear with you. They took off your clothes. They tied you to the rack. You are blindfolded. This is your body beneath the electric light you cannot see, here in the middle of the room. They surround you. Some give orders and others follow them. A doctor studies you and gives advice to the men who control the electric shocks and beat you. They all act together. This is not an improvised scene, and they are not novices. Some of them even brag about their studies abroad as if they were speaking of a graduate degree in engineering: Guatemala, Fort Benning, Panama. They are proud, and, you must admit, they know their work. *They are rigorous; they follow through with what they say to you.* And at this moment they tell you they are going to make you an invalid, that they are going to break your spine, that they are going to rape you, that they are going to pull everything you're hiding out of you and then they will kill you, or perhaps mutilate you and leave you blind.

Dawn approaches. You admitted from the beginning what you are: a guerrilla fighter. But you said that you had only just joined, that you didn't know the leaders or the safe house locations or the meeting points.

Who can endure so much?

You have to do something to rest for a bit from all this. You have to enter another terrain of combat. And so you come to the "confession, a story told to delay death."[5] And you scream. You tell them you'll take them to the room where you live with two other compañeros.

They begin to plan the operation. You think, you hope, that upon witnessing your detention, your compañeros will not have returned to that room.

They help put your clothes on and take you to a car that is then followed by two others. There is no other option. You guide them through the streets of Chilpancingo toward the room. The neighbors are asleep; the streets are deserted. No one sees you.

Your captors go upstairs. No one is in the room. They take the few things they find there, return to the cars, and then take you somewhere. They throw you on the floor and one of them begins to talk to you:

"You have to tell us how it was that the organization survived, how it re-organized, where the guerrillas hid, what capacity they have, who they are, what weapons they possess.

"Today we have an opportunity with you here and you

should tell us everything we want to know. You are the experi-
ment. We have enough time—and time is on our side—to find
out your identity. Legally we are not even going to acknowledge
who detained you. No one will investigate. We are experienced;
we have done this for many years. You bring us back a bit to the
1970s. We're going to do an update with you

"I'm just letting you know. There is nothing to hide
here. With you we're going to see if the guerrillas have
gotten better in the last twenty-two years. Have you all
developed something worthwhile, or are you still a bunch
of idiots? They are all going to speak: through you they
are going to speak. We have the time and we have the
means: tear out your fingernails, castration, needles, electric shocks, water torture, beatings, and strangulation.
That's how we'll begin the game: every two hours for as
long as you like. You decide. Here's the doctor. Starting
today it will be us against you. Starting today you will feel
the power of the State against you. Against you, because
we have you. And the only way to save yourself will be to
have us diminish one of your sessions a bit with what you
give us. Beyond that there will be no negotiation. What
do you say?"

"I don't say anything. I'm a prisoner."

"Do you recognize yourself as such?"

"Yes, yes I do."

"You are one of them?"

"Yes, I'm one of them."

"Why did you get into this?"

"It's a personal decision."

And they repeat all that they want from you: military
plans, safe house locations, guerrilla cells that you know,

who was with you in the park, where you all were going, what your rank is, how do the guerrillas find and transport arms, where do they store arms, who finances the guerrillas, who writes the communiqués, which writer or politician is behind you all, and where your central command is located.

Perhaps, without being entirely conscious of it, this interminable list has offended you, and you tell them that not even the President of the Republic has that kind of information. That unleashes the fury of the one who spoke to you and those who follow his orders. They kick and beat your entire body and within seconds you are curled on the floor and bleeding. They pick you up and take you again to the rack. They increase the voltage. They take out their anger on your body for a time that is impossible to measure until a voice tells them to stop for a moment. The pain in your bones, the exhaustion, the thirst.

It all repeats: the questions, the half answers, or the evasive or misleading answers, the pain, the destruction of your body and your emotions. Their language is also an instrument designed to break you, to make you surrender. But their questions don't seduce you. You think: *We do not speak the same language, and I don't mean the grammar, but the origin.*

After a session they tie you so that you can neither stand straight up nor sit down. As soon as you slip into sleep they wake you with kicks, punches, or by throwing water in your face. They do as they say: the sessions are every two hours. And the noun "session" burns, and in its embers lie the verbs break, destroy, fall, lose, and hurt.

They tore you from the world and brought you here

naked, bound, and blindfolded to where language crumbles on your tongue. The questions are echoes of the electric shocks; they meld with the cord used to strangle you; they join with the hands used to dislocate your shoulder. When you do not speak, your silence is the instant remaining before your bones shatter. When you speak, the words burrow into your thirst; they bite you and scratch against your throat. Yours is a rat-thirst that breaks into your veins and scurries throughout your body.

"Who were the other people with you?"

"They were journalists."

"We already know that. What we want to know is where were you going to take them for the interview."

You lie to them and they don't believe you. All of this that can't fit into words continues.

The questions. Again and again. Day after day. *How to explain the terror of them asking you the same questions for days on end? It destroys you. You feel like you've done the most exhausting physical labor. Ten or fifteen people asking you the same questions.* This is torture, nothing else. "In the modern technology of pain the question is always a component of pain itself. The question is never there for some pragmatic reason, that is, to elicit the revelation of a piece of information. The interrogation is not something that, once resolved to the torturer's satisfaction, would signify the end of the other's subjection to torture . . . [The] moment of interrogation is constitutive of the infliction of pain."[6]

They tell you that you are responsible for what they do to you because you won't tell them what they want to know, for not telling them what you know, for withholding the information they want. Yes, you are withholding everything, but you deny it. You say that you do not have the information they're after. But they don't believe you. They destroy you and destroy you again while they tell you it's your fault. From the very first minutes, during the first days, without being able to fully analyze your situation, inside you, inside the screams at the edges of which something true about who you are stands, your origin, your pride, you made the decision to refuse betrayal as an option. You decide to withhold everything and with your silence declare: This is who I am *and this is what I want to be.* You make the decision to fight.

They bring you food but you do not touch it, both out of hatred for them and out of a desire to step a bit closer to death. *You only drink water because the thirst is truly unbearable.*

They find the parking lot receipt in your pants and go for the car. You don't know this yet, but they have already interrogated and threatened the young man who parked your car and gave you the receipt. He said that he didn't know anything and then went and sought legal protection from a judge. They ask you about the car, a white Volkswagen. You say that you don't know anything about it. "Then why do you have the parking lot receipt in your pants pocket?" You lie, saying that your compañeros had given you the slip of paper and asked you to hold onto it without looking at it. They don't believe you, and the sessions continue every two hours.

If you were to think of your own history of pain, if you were to recall all the weariness, the hunger, the thirst, the worst physical exhaustion, the fevers, nausea, illnesses, burns, strikes, falls, cuts and scrapes, broken or dislocated bones, if you were to imagine that all of those pains already lived were combined and imposed upon your body at once, you would realize that not even that approaches what you feel now. And now it comes again.

You open your blindfolded eyes and look into the open throat of death. The shocks to your chest and the scream. You know that this throat is about to consume you. They beat your stomach and pour water up your nose. But first you'll have to pass through something you can only refer to with the word *hell*. They hit you in the face and blood fills your mouth. The water, the shocks to your genitals, and the scream. You want to find a way to escape, to buy time, to be able to think. They apply the shocks to your head: the explosion inside your skull. You see surrender take shape in your mind, and it scares you. You feel it inside you like invading bacteria. But death does not come. The plain of hell extends. There is no respite.

Five days pass like this. They say to you: "Five days have gone by and no one is looking for you. Why?" You lie. You tell them that you are an unknown, and they don't believe you. So one of them says to you: "*Look, asshole, you're already fucked. To put it plainly: we've already disappeared you. You are one more that disappears.*"

And you feel . . .

"*Now that we've seen how you are, from now on you will have two permanent guards, both officers with machine guns in hand. You'll remain blindfolded and with your hands and feet bound and chained to a wall. There is no way you can escape. We have the advantage and we're doing this to you because you won't talk. Or because you lie to us. The only thing you'll say now will be that you surrender and that we're the best. This is the price you'll pay for having dared to challenge the State. It's you against us. You have no chance. Have you decided to fight?*

"You're already done for. The time periods during which we could have taken you to jail have passed. We can't risk the tarnish to our reputation. And so, from this moment forward, you are ours for the time you have left to live. Which will not be much. Nothing can save you, unless you tell us everything we want to know."

This word: disappeared. They have so many ways of erasing you, "of trying to make you doubt the truth of your own life."[7] After five days, after every two hours, after only having felt a world of pain with no horizon, it is a word that breaks you, that wounds you inside, right to your identity. *It unmakes you.*

The human body cannot receive such violence and not scream. And your scream is this: you say you'll take them to a room in Acapulco where you live with two compañeros. They begin to mobilize in that instant. They tell you to put on your clothes, but you can't even stand up on your own. They have to help you get dressed. They take you to a vehicle to drive you to Acapulco.

You feel like a coward. The scream that, in the most minimal way, tried to alleviate your pain, now hurts you. You feel ashamed for having told them something true. It is a room in Acapulco and it has been five days since you were abducted. Once the words were said you hope that your compañeros have left the room. *They are supposed to do so within 48 hours.* You gave them five days. *That is a rule: houses are meant to be given to the torturers.*

But now, standing before the terrain opened by the word disappeared, in this place of pain and shame, you make a decision: *You don't want to kill me. You make me fight. Let's fight.*

You chose this. You knew that there were risks, but the risks did not dominate you. With that pride, *in the good sense*, you said: *No one will stop me. And this isn't some act of romanticism. I want this; I'm going to do it; I will achieve it.*

What was *this*? You weren't after blood, nor were you necessarily looking for war. It was to struggle—*luchar*—a verb now trivial in many ways, essential in others. For you it was and remains a verb of origin, of survival, and as such, indispensable.

You were born *in one of the poorest regions in the country. One supposes that these were the places where our ancestors sought refuge after the defeat of August 13, 1521, in the War of Tenochtitlán.* Your name contains your history: Andrés Tzompaxtle Tecpile. In other towns people asked you: *"Why do you have that name, that surname?"* And your response *was instinctive: "Well, yes, I have this name because I was not conquered. I have not been colonized and thus I have my language, my name, I retain my surname, my tradition."*

You were born on November 10, 1966, in Astacinga, Veracruz, one of eight brothers and sisters living in a one-room wooden house that your parents built by hand. You worked from early childhood and you enjoyed labor, your hands in the earth, taking care of the livestock. It was neither punishment nor exploitation. Your family ate what it produced. *Work was always a factor. The first activities you did were what your body would allow, like bringing water from the river or gathering firewood. The first things you have are your hands.* You can't wield work tools like the machete yet. *If you see the adults working, your father, your mother, for the same reasons you'll have to do so as well. First as play, later as a matter of education. And so,* you would say, *for us the earliest education is this work, from as soon as you can walk. You with your smallest pail going for water. Work is not suffering. Just as everyone eats, everyone has things to do.*

During your early childhood you never saw this thing they call *modernity. There are no highways, no electricity, nothing like that. No kindergarten. Once you were bigger, about seven or eight, you'd have to walk for an hour to reach the nearest school, or the nearest thing they call a school. You'll have to walk to do anything.* You were raised walking and running barefoot. Your *first huaraches would have come around the age of ten.* Yes, certain material things were lacking, certain technologies, or medicines. You all did not know *what a checkup, a doctor, a pill, or anti-parasite medications were.* But no one went hungry in your house. *This love of work, this respect for things, for corn, for beans, it forges your values. What you have to do is have principles. All that you should achieve will be the fruit of your efforts, not from seeing where you'll be given things, where to seek gifts, where to go asking. All this starts making you responsible, proud.*

But at school, the teachers would tell you: *You must learn to speak Spanish, that is the first step in bettering yourself, in getting ahead.* Bettering oneself? What is wrong with us as we are? What is wrong with speaking Náhuatl? Before going to the school you had always spoken your native language, you'd never even heard Spanish.

But you were just a child. And that's how you went to the sports tournament in San Juan Texhuacán. You were thirteen years old when you saw the children crying. Not one, but several. You and your compañeros approached them and asked them: Why are you crying? Did you all lose, or what happened? The children from Tehuipango told you how just the day before their families had been massacred. That was the first shock. *At first you don't understand. Why would they kill so many people? Then, this was close to your town. The question that assaults you is: What is to be done? In other words: We must avenge them. How? I don't know. But the idea is there. They must be avenged. What they did to them was unjust. It is not okay.*

You still did not know anything about the Army massacre of students on October 2, 1968, or the paramilitary massacre on June 10, 1971, both in Mexico City. You didn't know anything about what was happening in Guatemala, El Salvador, or Nicaragua. How could you have known *if one didn't have even the slightest idea where those places were located?* What you had heard a bit about were the histories and myths about the Guerrero teachers Genaro Vázquez and Lucio Cabañas. *That was something that did have an impact. One way or another, one learns of the existence of such groups.* And at thirteen years old, *upon hearing of that massacre, you first feel the call to seek out Lucio the teacher.* You had heard about him for the first time when you were six or seven years old: a government official had taken a photograph of Lucio Cabañas to your town with the ambition of being able to arrest him were he to make an appearance there. But *instead of saying we need to find him,* the mayor took the photograph, put it in a frame, *and hung it behind his little desk.*

At the age of eighteen, you made your decision. You said: *I want this.* And you didn't base your decision on books or films, the histories of Che or Ho Chi Minh, the images of the piled bodies in Tlatelolco, or the texts or theories of long-dead Germans or Russians. From the age of thirteen you were driven by the idea of looking for Lucio Cabañas, someone with whom you could join to *avenge the crimes that had been committed. Lucio was the refuge that you could seek out without knowing where Guerrero is.*

Why struggle? When asked in Spanish in Mexico City, Monterrey, Guadalajara, or Acapulco, this question does not look out upon the same horizon as when asked in Náhuatl in the Zongolica mountains or in Ñu Savi in the Costa Chica. It is never the same question twice. It is always a social question. Profoundly intimate, it always has social veins within its solitude. And though asking it is not the same in 1968, 1988, 1996, or 2014, the differences between moments when the question is posed do not cut the roots of time inside the question. It shares histories even inside its solitude.

Why struggle? The question will never have a definitive answer, a pre-established answer, or a correct answer. It must be faced afresh and in its full dimension every time it is asked. And whosoever confronts the question may have to do so many times over the course of their life. To ask it will always be intimate and social at the same time. This multiple nature of the question invites conversation, which is another way of joining the solitary and the social, assuming that the one who opens the question "why?" knows how to listen.

And so, why? It is difficult to explain, of course, but you would say that *we were never going to accept submission just because. Our idea has not been colonized. We're as decolonized as we've always been. We have memory. So it was not some political influence, but rather our tradition of resisting domination, of continuing to rebel. It becomes a characteristic, a tradition, and that is something that perhaps many people do not understand. The State, far from thinking of all this, asks: "Where is the manual you learned from?" "Which school did you go to?" But there are no manuals, no schools, there is only life, nothing more.*

Life. Tradition. *Omeyocan, toltecáyotl, tlachinollan. Our duality, our philosophy, our blood. We are aware,* you would say, *of our history. Others came before us. Today we are here, but tomorrow there will be others. We want to live well. But, what does live well mean to us? To live well means to live in harmony with nature. To live well means not contaminating our rivers and oceans, not cutting down our forests. It means eating well and without so many chemicals. To produce our food. Exchange our food. We don't want palaces and buildings, nor to fill everything with concrete and contaminants. It means to live without looting. We don't want to live accumulating and hoarding. We don't want to exploit others. We don't want to destroy the land, because it is our life. We don't want to damage it more than they already have. We want to live well; we want to conserve the land because part of the life of that land is us. Our thought is different; it is not the same. In this plan of saving many things, the species itself is saved. And even despite everything they do, they themselves are saved; their lives are safe. That's why we are doing this. For all these values: for this dignity, for this decency, for this feeling. More than thought, it is feeling. More than political ideology, it is humanism.*

As an eighteen-year-old Nahua man from the Zongolica mountains, a descendant of those who survived the War of Tenochtitlán, you found the survivors of the war against Lucio Cabañas and the Party of the Poor and you went with them and joined the guerrilla movement. At first those were enthusiastic, even impulsive times. *You believe in this; it is what you want; it is your life; you make it your life, not in some fanatical act, but in an act of conscience from which you continue to learn by completing tasks, forging yourself.*

You would say that *later one realizes the stigma that the State deploys to condemn this social struggle. Because that is what we are, we are fighters for justice, nothing else. We're not fighting against hunger anymore, but against the war of extermination, the war of invasion, the war disguised in many forms: as education, as politics, as culture, as repression. So one supposes that given all these characteristics of extreme poverty, of malnutrition, of no standing before the law, of no schools existing, well, then one supposes that those who haven't died yet have survived in order to live through an early death. So if you struggle and become something, it is twice the shock. First, because you didn't die, and that's a challenge. But, well, according to the State, you should be there without any capacity for critical thought. That's another challenge—for them—that we continue to live and think on our own. They say: "How is it possible that they haven't died but they still haven't lost the capacity for thought?" But, in addition to thinking, one decides to do something, one decides to fight.*

In a context such as yours, to struggle is to be, to live.

Let's recall: The lands known now as the Americas were violently invaded. The invaders declared themselves conquerors and built the institutions necessary to administer the success of their invasion. You would say: *The history of our country is a history of plunder.* The fundamental and constitutive act of those institutions was to decree that all the original human inhabitants of these lands, and the human inhabitants from afar later captured and brought to these lands, would be defined and treated as slaves, animals, property. The logic of that decree was articulated through the creation and murderous imposition of racial categories. Those institutions have been many times modified, but they have never been dismantled. The simultaneous ontological, epistemic, and corporeal violence of the invasion, racism, and slavery is at the root of the institutions that today we call the State, law, capitalism.[8] *They continue to massacre the massacred, shielding themselves in something they call the law.* State power may be exercised through a court, a legislature, the police, the army, but it is always a power that constructs supremacy through invasion, racism, patriarchy, and slavery. Just as one's bones hold one's parents' DNA in the cells' architecture, contemporary political institutions code the violence of genocide and slavery in the architecture of their power.

Up to our present day, millions of human beings navigate daily through societies and institutions that deny their humanity, their names, their languages, their lands, their histories, their visions of the world, their longings, their lives. You would say: *We are nothinged. We are poverty statistics, squalor statistics. We are not citizens, we are not good consumers.* To struggle also means not accepting these things. *In addition to thinking, one decides to do something, one decides to fight.*

And this is what you were doing, a young Nahua guerrilla fighter carrying out the task of leading a group of well-known journalists to the mountains for an interview with the state commanders of the EPR. Your ranking officers told you to go unarmed so that the journalists would not report seeing you with weapons, and thus give government officials a pretext for saying, "Look how violent they are." This was a strange strategy, considering how those same leaders had planned the armed attacks of two months before.

But you and your compañero, both combatants, obeyed your orders. The journalists had spent two days going from one place to another. Acapulco, Tierra Colorada, Chilpancingo. They had not seen either of you before and would not have been able to recognize you in public. In each place someone approached them and gave them a piece of paper with a map and directions for the next meeting place. The rules of clandestinity were rigorous and tedious, and you all did not trust the reporters. Sometimes distrust can lead to excess: *By being so careful you end up being careless.*

The journalists did not pass through Tierra Colorada on their way back from Acapulco. You had been waiting there, hidden, to make sure no one was following the reporters. You did not suspend the interview when the reporters did not follow this security protocol. You and your compañero went to Chilpancingo and parked your car there. You put the parking lot receipt in your pants pocket and took a taxi to Zumpango del Río, some twenty kilometers from Chilpancingo.

You saw the journalists walking in circles, confused, in the plaza. They had been told to look for "a man in a baseball cap near the kiosk." That man would pass close to the journalists and they would then follow a few meters behind him. The problem was that on that October 25, there were a number of men with baseball caps near the kiosk. While the journalists looked for the contact—who walked right by them several times—you saw three men sitting on the fence in a corner of the plaza. They seemed odd to you, but you didn't say anything.

At last the journalists recognized the contact and followed behind him. You and your compañero were in the rearguard position, following behind the journalists. You realized that someone was following you, one of the three men you saw sitting on the fence. You stopped and pointed him out to your compañero. You even asked: *"Is he one of ours?" "I don't know," your compañero answered, "let's let him catch up to us."*

The man passed you both; he even said hello. Then the other two men passed you both. You two began to walk again. A bit further along, the fight started, the third man took out his pistol, you struggled with him, your compañero took off running, and then all three men took you down. The other guerrillas and the journalists all escaped. Only you remained behind with the three men. Their trucks arrived shortly thereafter.

They take you to Acapulco handcuffed, lying on the floor of a vehicle you recognize as a van or a Suburban. Upon arriving they sit you up in the seat, with a pistol to your head. You show them the room. A number of them get out and take up positions around the different exits of the apartment building. They keep you inside the vehicle, at gunpoint. You listen to the operation over the radio they use to communicate. They ask you what name you use with the men who live in this room. You tell them a false name.

After a short time they all come back, furious. The room was empty. They spoke to the owner of the building who told them that the renters in that room had moved out that very day, at around one in the afternoon; that is, just a few hours ago.

If you had told them about the room yesterday, or even earlier this morning, two of your compañeros would now be torn from the world.

They come back enraged and begin to beat you there in the vehicle. They tell you they're going to take you to a "branch office" they have here on the outskirts of Acapulco to reinitiate your sessions.

They tell you: *"You gave us the room knowing that they had already left it."* They tie you to the rack and begin again: electric shocks using cables connected to a car, beatings, strangulation, suffocation, blows to your spine. You want to die. One of them squirts water up your nose and you spit it back at him, to provoke him. You try not to scream, hoping thus to faint, to take a step toward death. You've decided. Soon you feel *something so, so comfortable, a lovely sound.* You begin to rest. You see a colorful field and then feel a punch to your face and hear a voice that screams: *"Wake up motherfucker! We're torturing you! Throw water on him. He's dying, for fuck's sake. We don't want him to die. Let him rest."*

They take you off the rack. Your legs can't hold you and you fall to the floor. They tell you to put on your clothes. You can't. They stand you up, dress you, handcuff you, bind you with a heavy chain and throw you in a corner. For the first time in five days they let you sleep.

You wake to pain. *You feel like you are dying, like you cannot move. Two hours go by and your body stays the same.*

They begin again. Now they go after you with a single objective: They want you to physically describe the men who lived in the room. They are focused. They only repeat that question. The electric shocks, the blows to your spine, to your head. The pain. And you give. Again with the shame eating at you from inside, and pain as the only and implacable reality: You give. But not entirely. You give, but without completely surrendering, without relinquishing your decision to fight: Once again you deliver a story to hold back death. So you mix real features—assuming that they would already have some physical description from having asked the owner of the apartment building and the neighbors—with false features. You make up a scar for one of them, and a necklace for the other.

After that they bring you a complete meal three times a day with meat, beans, tortillas, orange juice, bread, and water. You don't trust them and so you eat the minimum: the bread and the tortillas. They insult you and threaten you. They continue with the sessions.

Two weeks after your disappearance they ask you for the first time: "Who is commander Rafael?" From that question a certain relief emerges: Your compañeros must be demanding that the military deliver you, alive and publicly, to the civilian authorities. But you, by instinct, by brute reflex, you tell them that you don't know who that is.

"You are commander Rafael."

And, yes, you are. That is your alias, even though you do not have that rank, but you respond: *That's not me.*

"Well then, why are they calling you that?"

"I guess they have to invent a name. It's logical. I haven't gone back, haven't appeared. That's not my name. If the

description of the events, the place, and all that coincide, then yes, it's me, but that name is something they're throwing out. That's not me."

You know very well that they don't believe you. You know that your response is futile, and that it will bring you suffering, and still you do it on purpose. They also lie. They tell you that the EPR communiqué calls you a commander. You don't believe that. Your compañeros would not give you that rank, knowing that it would bring you harm. The communiqués always identify you as a "combatant," but the perpetrators of your suffering say something different. They say that you are a "commander" and you deny it—in this case truthfully—you deny the rank.

One of them says: *"We're going to work you over more now because you were deceiving us. And you've got a rank, here it is. Look, tell me, how many days have you been here? You've been here many days now. What is the difference between you, a nobody—you yourself say you're a nobody—and a commander? There's no difference. They're the same."*

You're able to say, *"No,"* and he cuts you off saying: *"For us that's what you are. That is the problem. And that's what we're going to call you from now on."*

You think: *Well, if only others would honor me and not these idiots.*

For the enemy, no matter what you do, even if you are just a sympathizer, you are a guerrilla. In fact, they can even blow it all out of proportion and say, "You are the biggest badass of all," or "You are the best." For them there is only one level: They're all the same. You can't just put on a stupid face and hope they say, "Ah, this one doesn't know much, let's take it a little bit easier on him."

Over these past few days they have kept looking in Acapulco for the compañeros from the room. The building owner told them that the renters left in a moving van. They went to all the small moving companies in the neighborhood until they found the driver who had taken them. They made the driver take them to the building to which the compañeros had moved. They set up a surveillance operation, but they didn't know which apartment the compañeros had moved to: the driver had not gone inside the building and didn't see the apartment.

They take you out in the pre-dawn hours. You go down the twenty-three stairs and they take you to a steep street. They put you in a truck with tinted windows and take you to a street in a working-class neighborhood. They take off your blindfold. At first you can't see well at all and you tell them so. Don't worry, they say, your eyes will adjust. And indeed, little by little, your vision improves. Four of them stay in the truck with you. They also have people on the street corners and beside all the building exits. They point out a large black doorway and tell you to watch carefully all of the people who come out through that doorway. One of the men in charge, one who has administered your pain for approximately two weeks, tells you not to let him down. He tells you that as soon as they grab the others they are going to let you go, because "you've already suffered a lot." And he pats you on the back a few times.

Dawn is breaking but your eyes have yet to grow accustomed to the light. You have difficulty seeing into the distance. You see someone exit the black doorway and walk toward the corner and you think it might be the *compa* you know, but you can't see him well. You don't say anything.

Two hours later the same man returns and enters the building. After just a bit a man exits, running, with a black briefcase in hand. You don't recognize him; you don't say anything; and they don't move. The man with the black briefcase takes the first cab that passes by and leaves. You think that it might have been someone from the organization, or someone visiting the people you know who detected the operation and took off running. You really don't know who he was.

Around noon you see your compañero—the same man you thought you had recognized in the early morning—as he exits the building again. He is wearing shorts, a Selena T-shirt and the tennis shoes that you had given him a few weeks before. *The compa is about a meter away as he walks by, and the guy is as calm as can be.*

"Some guy's leaving."

"I can't see," you say, and you lean toward the window seeing quite clearly, but you repeat: *"I don't know, I can't see well."*

He comes back, but then almost immediately leaves again.

"Look, he's leaving again."

And he is leaving again. When he walks by again you think: *This is the second time he's passed by, they are baiting me with him. They already have him, they're just making him walk by on purpose to see if I'm really collaborating or just playing the fool. Well, if that's the case, so be it. I'm never going to point him out. If they've already got him, then they've got him, but not because of me.*

He walks to the corner and stops. He crosses to the other corner and stops again. You look off in another direction. Fear rises up and surges inside you. In your peripheral vision you see the compañero take off running and they don't do anything, waiting for the order from the man sitting next to you in the truck. They don't pay the compa any mind and he leaves.

Minutes later they give the order to return. You don't know if they've become tired or if they realized that the compañeros have already left. They go back to the base. They take you up the twenty-three stairs. One of them says to you: *"Well, that would have saved you. We had them in our hands, but you didn't want it. You let them leave. You've let everyone escape from the places you've taken us."*

You think: obviously, asshole, that's the point. And then, again the beatings, the electric shocks, the suffocation, the threshold. But now the parameters of the combat have been established. Now the laboratory of pain is the given, the air you breathe. The fight will not involve wires or fists. It will be something other. You will fight with facts and lies and their infinite possible combinations. *This is the only recourse you find.*

You have been *reduced to nothing, but inside there is pride, arrogance. The reality of your body no longer obeys you, but this idea of the fight . . .* You think: *I'm now a part of this world, this is my world, this fucking hell, and it is up to me how it will all finish. But if you get clumsy even for thirty seconds, I'm gone, I'll surprise you, I'll take you. I will choose my end. How and when.*

You decide this. It has nothing to do with hope. Hope can be a fantasy, a lie, a sedative, but hope can also lead to its opposite. It is better to prepare daily for the worst. Here dignity rejects hope.[9] You seek refuge in the darkness behind your blindfold where you will manipulate them, where you will beat them. It becomes an obsession: escape. Not to wait for them to free you. Not to wait for anything from them. This is up to you. Escape.

But then comes the hour of the rack, the hour of the questions, when they repeat: *You must realize that the only thing you have is the time left before you die.*

And then faced with the pain you think: *Fuck, man, this is reality, and it is theirs.* Your body is the realm over which they try to exhibit their domination, their control. And yes, "the physical evidence goes against you, you're so weak, so sick and so tormented you think, if you can think . . . I am these stinking wounds; I am this festering sore. That is what you have to fight with. And it's goddamn difficult; because whenever they feel like it, they replenish the physical evidence that goes against you."[10] *But all right,* you think, *I'll take refuge in what I'm imagining.*

And so it begins. You invent meetings that you had scheduled where some of your compañeros—assuming they had not heard of your disappearance—might show up. Neither the meetings nor the people exist. They plan their operations, gathering their guns, spreading out in the streets, stationed in their different cars. They wait. And you sit inside the truck with a gun to your head, but with your eyes making contact with the light and without electricity coursing through your body. On the one hand you half wait, you hold on to a fantasy that someone passing by randomly on the street could recognize you through the tinted windows and tell your compañeros who could then denounce your being held incommunicado and use the media to put pressure on the government to publicly account for you. A fantasy. But on the other hand, it refreshes you to see them invest their resources and move all over the city pursuing ghosts you create for them *while at the same time diminishing the pain a little*. Such are your small victories. Even though you return, always without prisoners, and they take out their frustration on your body, your being. And like the water drops falling on the bound prisoner's face: the questions, *the quantity of things they repeat. That they could say to you a hundred times, for example, "Tell me your name." And it's not a matter of hours, but days, and weeks, and months*.

Until one day, some two months after your capture, *they come in triumphant* to the room where you are handcuffed, tied, and blindfolded.

"At last, asshole: now you're really fucked."

You think: *What do you mean "now," it has been quite a while . . .*

"Your lies are over, asshole. You're done. Because now . . . now we know who you are. And we have something here that will interest you." He pauses and then continues: *"We've got your wife and also your kids."*

The impact is so overwhelming that really no . . . You tremble and feel like, yes, now you are truly fucked. You think: *How did they find out about them? How could they have found out? What happened?* But your immediate reaction is to deny everything: *"No, I don't have a wife and kids."*

"Are you going to tell us the truth, yes or no?"

"Well, what are you talking about? I don't know."

"Look, I went to a human rights organization and spoke with a woman who is your wife. She's not in trouble, she's not mixed up in this. We know that. But since you haven't been home, she's looking for you and asking for help there at the

human rights organization. She wants to find you. I spoke with her, and she told me she's looking for you."

You think: *Yes, they could do something like that, but she wouldn't. What would have led her to do that? Who might have suggested it to her? I don't know. But knowing how murderous these people are, they wouldn't wait one second to bring her here in front of me. I don't think they have her. No, they don't have her. Perhaps something is happening. They know something, but they don't know everything. If they did know, they'd have my wife and kids right here, right now, and they'd torture me together with them. There is no doubt about that. If I admit I have a wife and children, I could harm them.*

Everything is a fight, war. You insist that you are not married and do not have children.

"So you're saying I'm a liar?"

"No, I'm not saying you're lying, but I can't admit to something that doesn't exist."

"Ok. Then, tell me, why is this woman saying you're her husband?"

"Well, let's think of the possibilities."

"Okay. Tell me."

"One possibility is that the organization is looking for me. They haven't found me. Let's say that a woman in the struggle or some volunteer pretends to be my wife to see if that way the government accounts for me. It could be that."

"Sure, it could be something like that. But what are you if you're not a man?"

"No. I'm a man, but I'm not married."

"Well, just in case, so there isn't any doubt about whether or not you are her husband, I'm going to bring her here. We're going to bring her and see if she recognizes you."

"Okay. Sure."

But she wouldn't do that. And if she did, it would be stupid. And if someone advised her to do it, then they were stupid. Imagine seeing your child tortured. If it feels awful when they do it to someone else, with your child . . . No, no, I can't imagine it.

You think: *They don't have her. The organization must have made something public, but they don't have her. Because, honestly, if they had her, they wouldn't waste a moment. They'll use everything they can.*

But the impact of the moment when they told you they had your family wrecked you. You think: *And to top it all off, I'm still alive.*

Someone comes to tell you that you have suffered a lot. That he even thinks the government is behaving badly, that he's thinking of looking for a contact with the EPR so he can help them. He says he is studying law and this is just a day job in the meantime. He offers to take any note or message you write to someone in the organization or your family, so that they'll know you're still alive.

Another tells you that they'll be taking you somewhere else. He admits that they have tortured you, "but with moderation." He says that it is his job, his obligation. He's worried about you. He says, "I've been your buddy and haven't mistreated you too much, but the ones who will take over from me, they are true killers." You listen to him curled on the floor, handcuffed, tied, blindfolded, wearing the same clothes they abducted you in and accompanied by a choir of incessant pains all over your body, all over your being. He says: "If you go before them you'll realize that what we did to you amounted to gentle caresses.

But if what I've just told you matters to you, you can tell me what you've been hiding. If you collaborate with me, I'll take you where no one can touch you."

You thank him for his kind offer and then tell him: "Unfortunately, I'm not hiding anything." But inside you, his proposal and his calm tone of voice, as insidious as it may be, awoke in you the longing for someone to defend you, to help you. Just a longing that signals what is not there, precisely that which is furthest away from you. *No, you are not saved. You are his enemy, and about this there is no uncertainty. They can use you for a bit, wring you out, but you'll never matter to them unless you become one of them. That's why you'd have to prove your conversion with acts and not just proclaim it in words. That is, only if you started to lead them to people.*

And thus, they destroy you.

You think: *For us there is no honor in that. That is something for cowards. That is not for me. Maybe it's not so bad crawling on all fours. But no. That's not in my language. That is not within the conditions that I can accept. I have a very different concept of life, of how to be, and they aren't going to change that just because they want to, because they try to impose a change on me. That would make me a puppet, an object to be controlled, a domesticated individual to be programmed. They could demand: "Say this," and I'd say it; "Do this," and I'd do it. And thus, what would such an individual become if not one of them, a person without identity, without conscience, without dignity? Such an individual, even when they do not die, would have just met their death, paradoxically, even though they say they are alive. That is the difference. Yes, I want to live. But not like that. I love life, profoundly, but not at that price.*

They bring other prisoners and torture them in front

of you, or in the next room. This frightens you and rips at you in a different way, even though you've been through the same. *It feels even worse when they do it to someone else, because you don't hear yourself. But the act of listening to the other . . . and then they do it to you . . . that is an effective method. It scares you.*

Maybe they don't even know what to do with you. They give you blank pieces of paper and tell you to write your history with the guerrillas, to name the opposition politicians and intellectuals behind the EPR, to confess which military operations you participated in, and to write that you regret it all. They say that they are going to film you and play the recording on television and the radio. *We're going to help you,* they say.

"*If you already have it written, you can make it public,*" you tell one of them.

"*No. No, you have to write it and appear in the video.*"

"*I can't. That doesn't suit me; that's not me. You make a mistake in choosing me. That's not who I am.*"

"*Then you'll be fucked.*"

"*Well, here I am. I've been here for a long time now. That's nothing new.*"

But it is part of the fight. Afterward you tell him yes, you'll write, and you write about events that already appeared in the news. But you write precisely about the events in which you did not participate. It is all part of the fight: They tear up the sheets of paper, they give you new ones and tell you to do it again.

They come for you one day. They untie you, lead you out of the room, and take you to a large vehicle, a Suburban or some other kind of van. They do not speak to you. After a bit the vehicle starts to travel at high speed. You're on a highway. Are they taking you on another operation? Are they taking you somewhere to kill you? They exit the highway and come to a stop. They don't take you out of the vehicle. You do not know where you are. Time moves in slow motion in the darkness of the blindfold. They get back in, start the vehicle and get back on the highway. After a while they repeat the same thing. This time you hear a large gate opening, but they do not drive through the gate. They get back in and start off again, driving for about two hours. They stop again, at a tollbooth it seems. You can hear the constant noise of car engines. You tell them you need to go to the bathroom. They neither answer you nor take you to a bathroom. They keep driving and after a while you can hear city sounds. They stop a lot and you think it must be for traffic lights. Could they be taking you to some jail? You've gone through the southern part of Mexico City, but perhaps they are going to North Jail. But no. They leave the city. You think: the maximum-security prison in *Almoloya? Well, even that would be an improvement.*

Then they come to a cold place. They stop and one of them gets out and speaks to someone. You hear a large gate opening, the vehicle drives through it and seems to go around in circles a few times, going over speed bumps before stopping. They take you out of the car and lead you about twenty meters. You hear the sound of water in a canal. They open a door and put you in an extremely cold room where you can hear the sound of an air-conditioning unit. They sit you down and tie your handcuffs to a metal structure. You think you might be in Almoloya. But that thought does not last long. The door opens and an older man—gauging by the sound of his voice—comes inside.

He tells you, "We brought you here to kill you." But he offers to save you if you tell him what you're hiding. He tells you that he's been doing this for more than twenty years, that he fought against Lucio Cabañas and Genaro Vázquez and now you're "one more." He says that he respected Lucio Cabañas because Cabañas showed his face, but those in the EPR do not show theirs.

"You're in our hands now, so you'll start to tell us everything."

"Well, I've already said everything."

"Oh, come on. I can save you. I can help you."

And you think: *If they publicly accounted for me today, even if they freed me, it would be humiliating. Why am I here? Why so many months? What have I missed? Surely another in my shoes would have done things better. Maybe even escaped already. Me . . . since the moment of my abduction they've won every battle. They've had every advantage. I haven't talked, but they have won. What I need to do now is something that hurts them. But, how? What do I have? I don't have shit. I have nothing, no advantage.*

You start listening to everything. The different sounds of animals: roosters, burros, dogs. You are outside of any city limits. You hear explosions sometimes in the afternoons, perhaps dynamite or something like that. You think there may be gravel mines nearby. Sometimes you can hear the shouts of children playing: Could there be some kind of apartment building near? But above all you listen to them. The ones who sleep in the room next to yours, the ones who guard you day and night. One of them snores.

Another always flips through the television channels. Another leaves the television on when, it seems, he has fallen asleep. Another screams at you anytime you make a sound. Another either doesn't realize it when you make sounds, or doesn't say anything.

When you are alone in the room you lift up the blindfold just a little bit with your finger. You don't know if there is a video camera in the room, so you do it little by little. You let in just a bit of light and start to see the room in pieces: there is one small window and another window with Persian glass panes. You begin to toy with the handcuffs, all the time. Night and day. Here they have you handcuffed one hand to a metal grid. You become obsessed with being able to pull your hand out of the handcuffs. Pulling and twisting against the handcuffs becomes the physical reflex corresponding to the word that haunts you now: *escape, escape, escape. That word.*

They've isolated you here. The sessions are no longer every two hours, but sporadic. You go days without speaking. You exercise your jaw, but even so when they interrogate you your mouth feels clumsy and painful. You exercise your body by contracting and releasing your muscles, one by one. You exercise by pushing against the wall *with the fantasy that one day it will fall down, but that is just a fantasy.* But when they see you, you exaggerate your physical degradation. They give you water and you grab the bottle with trembling hands. They take you blindfolded to the bathroom and you bump into the walls on purpose and they berate you for not learning how to walk. They speak to you and you pretend to be asleep until they hit you. Now they only give you bread and water, even though they leave plates of food nearby, perhaps to see if you try to reach the food, or just to make you suffer with the smells of cooked meals.

You fight with the handcuffs until one night you're able to pull your hand out. You stand up. You approach the window and in that instant a car pulls up. You throw yourself back on the floor and stick your hand back through the handcuffs. It is hard to get your hand back through. One of them comes in and asks you what you're doing. You pretend to be asleep. He jerks the chain of your handcuffs, walks around the room and then leaves.

One night you are listening to the seven o'clock news with Lolita Ayala. They are talking about the case of General Jesús Gutiérrez Rebollo, Mexico's first federal "drug czar," who was himself accused of and sentenced for drug trafficking. Then they announce that, after "exhaustive investigations" the police found an EPR safe house in Acapulco. A strange chill hits your bones. Ayala says that the police did not arrest any members of the EPR but confiscated military uniforms, boots, "subversive instructional films," and other things. And you think: *That is the house I was responsible for.* Moreover: the house where you lived with your wife and small children. The chill clenches down on your bones. That house, you think, *was the symbol of my life, I made it into the symbol of my life. I traded that house for my life. Because if I had given them that house, then I think they would have publicly presented me; that would have been a serious blow against us,* against the EPR. *They would have paraded me* before the media *if I had given them that house. But I didn't, and I never would have. And so, what was all this time, all this suffering for if the compañeros left the goddamned house with everything in it? It is only a matter of hours before I'm subjected, again, to all the interrogation.*

With the chill comes your anger against your own compañeros. *What happened?* Why didn't they clear out the house? Why didn't they remove everything? How did the police find the house?

And you think: *The police didn't find it. I didn't give them any indication of that house. The only possibility is that the compañeros did abandon the house. They went and then left it. I had three months of rent paid in advance. The owner must have gone to ask for the rent for the fourth month. After the three months had passed, she must have gone inside and seen everything that was there. And then the most logical thing is that she'd call the police. She has witnesses who can testify that she rented the house to others. The owner—it was her; she turned in the house. The police didn't find it.*

The next day they come and take the blindfold off your eyes. They are not wearing masks.

"Do you have anything to tell me?"

"Um, okay. Yes, I'll tell you something."

"What?"

"Well, the house that they just found in Acapulco, I did know about that house. I didn't want to give it to you because I thought it would be empty. As you know, when someone is taken prisoner, the least the compañeros can do is take everything out of the house. I didn't turn it over because I thought if you all were to find it empty, you'd think I was mocking you. And, well, that wouldn't bode well for me. If I'd known that they weren't going to clear it out, I would have turned it over, and maybe that would have saved me. But, well, it's too late now."

"How do you know that we have the house?"

"Well, you do have it."

"Let's suppose we have it. What was in that house?"

You tell them that the house had uniforms, a television set, a video camera, a typewriter, boots, and two 9mm pistols.

"Who used the house?"

"I don't know. They had protocols so that I wouldn't see them."

"And why didn't you ever take a look?"

"Because it was against the rules, no? I didn't have any reason to break the rules."

"You obey the rules?"

"Fuck. Okay, well, like you've just said, we didn't even get that right. I know that there is no . . . but, I want you all to know that . . . maybe that was what I was hiding. And it's okay, I know I'm done."

"Whom did you live with there?"

"Well, I lived with the young woman who pretended to be my wife, but she wasn't. That was just a cover."

"And this photo?"

He shows you a photograph of your family. *How was this damn photo there?!*

"It's your wife."

"Yes, it's my wife."

"Why didn't you confess this before?"

"Because it's not her fault, she was just accompanying me."

"Where can we find her?"

"I don't know."

"Do you think she's still with them?"

"I doubt it. The most likely thing is that she got frightened and went to look for work in another city."

"And do you know why I took off your blindfold? Do you know why I'm not wearing a mask?"

"I don't know, but I can guess . . . "

"What?"

"Well, it's the end."

"Yes, it is the end. I mean, all the time you had us running around like fools, all that time is over. This is the consequence."

"No worries."

"Really?"

"No, no problem."

"Why?"

"Because we're on different sides and usually when it comes to the end one doesn't get the chance to talk about it. This is one of those chances, or at least that's how I see it."

He even gives you his hand to shake.

They flood your room and the chill strikes you. They come back the next day and tell you that they have your wife. The fear hits your bones. You are blindfolded again. You hear the sound of a person approaching. You hear someone walk into the room, perhaps a woman, for this person wears high-heels and walks well in them. *You hear them lead her into the room and then back out.* Is it your compañera? *No, it's not her.* And you think: *It is the owner of the house.* They must have brought her here from Acapulco to confirm whether or not you are the person who rented her house. She would have told them yes. Or could they have just led a woman in high-heels into the room so that you would think they have your wife?

This leaves you pensive. *You feel a lack of will, of initiative, for not having tried to escape yet. And not some bullshit of throwing yourself at the door, but something where you really have some advantage. But, what advantage? You don't know where you are, nor in what kind of facility.* You don't want to keep going like this. You think of killing yourself, but that seems cowardly. The other option is *to provoke them into killing you.* But one thing is clear to you: *I am not willing to stay like this any longer. I will not live like this, for this is not life, it's not right. I too can decide how this ends. In fact, I will be the one who decides. Let's accelerate this end then. That's what I will do; I have no other choice; I can't see any other possibility. I think I've lacked will. I've been struck by cowardice. It is as if I were waiting for an opportunity, but a comfortable one, like if the door were to open toward a tunnel leading out of here. But, well, that's not possible. So let's play the final hand, let's end this.*

You choose this end. It is not suicide: It is combat.

You've eaten little and today decide not to eat. You haven't defecated in three days and you want to avoid it now. If they were to take you off to the toilet then they would have to remove and replace your handcuffs and you'd run the risk of them putting them back on tighter. Right now they are being a bit lazy. You've been testing them constantly. But you can't hold back the need to urinate so you grab the bottle they use to bring you water and urinate in it. Someone walks in and sees you.

"Why are you pissing . . . ?"

"I didn't want to bother. It is just piss. I'll throw it out the next time I have to go."

He asks you if you need to go now. You say no. In response he hits you a few times and leaves. You sweat, but not because of the punches. *The punches don't hurt; you've grown accustomed to them.* You sweat from the fear that they'll tighten your handcuffs.

That night you try to sleep in lapses. In the predawn hours you try to listen to the television. It has been a while since anyone has changed the channel. You make a quiet sound. No one shouts at you. You think: *I'll use the most minimal carelessness in my favor.* You try to remove your hand from the handcuffs. It gets stuck between the bones of the wrist and thumb. You pull and pull until it comes out all of a sudden, tearing off a piece of skin. You lift up the blindfold and walk toward the bathroom and start to remove the glass panes from the window. And then, again, you see a vehicle approach.

You throw yourself to the floor and try to put your hand back in the handcuffs, but you can't. As hard as you try, your hand gets stuck. You put your blindfold back on and lie on the floor, lying over your hand, holding onto the cuffs. One of them comes in and screams at you. You pretend to be asleep. He kicks you and you curl up and wince, exaggerating the pain. He kicks you a few more times and then leaves. You wait a few long minutes. There is no turning back. If he comes back in, what will you do? You could tackle him. You could jump through the window. You could provoke him into killing you. *All the options lead to the same ending.*

Your body is hot. You feel, contrary to logic, to the image of your withered body, and to any reasonable expectation, invincible. "Freedom resides in whoever tries to reach it."[11] Freedom resides *in whoever is prepared to face the end, to declare oneself dead in order to live.*

You remove the blindfold and stand up again, shaking. You take another two panes out of the Persian window, place them on the floor, and jump out. Neither your legs nor your arms have the strength to break your fall and you hit your head. That hurts. But you don't make a sound. No glass broke. It is *a movement so perfect that you'd never have been able to achieve it even if you'd practiced.*

You stand up and begin walking. It is still dark, but they have just played reveille. You see a wire fence, possibly electrified. You see a number of buildings and realize that you are not in a little house, nor a neighborhood, nor an apartment building, nor a police base. You are in a military base. *That's why they were so confident.* You walk and see a soldier approaching. You raise up your hands in pure reflex, but the soldier does not raise his weapon; he does not seem to pay any attention to you. You keep you arms up, as if you had been stretching, out for morning exercise. The soldier passes and greets you, *good morning.* You look around. There are a number of residential buildings and playing fields. You see two civilian-dressed people walking across one of the fields, toward the fence. They arrive at a place where it is easy to jump over the fence, and they jump over it. You follow them.

THE SILENCES

"THIS ISN'T A DEAD MAN'S book," Andrés Tzompaxtle Tecpile told me one day. "This book is about someone alive. The book won't tell the whole story." When he said that, I understood that the book could not tell the whole story, and also that Tzompaxtle would not tell me his whole story. At one point he told me: "It is indescribable. I can't understand nor remember everything that happened to me." And at another point he told me that he always tells the story differently: "I think that every time I tell the story some things from the hidden damage will come out, things that represent the permanence of that hidden damage, or perhaps the healing of it . . ."

Before beginning, a writer here faces two fields of inaccessible information: one blocked by an act of will, the other blocked by trauma and the inevitable and unpredictable fractures of memory. At least there was no doubt about this: Many things would remain unknown. Thus uncertainty was accompanied by honesty from the beginning.

During a journalism conference at the 2012 Guadalajara International Book Fair, Francisco Goldman, author of *The Art of Political Murder*, said: "Impunity is the freedom of expression of the killers. If you aren't afraid that

101

someone will grab and punish you, then you can plan and carry out a murder like a theater production."[1] The work of one who seeks to solve a case, one who seeks justice—especially concerning acts of murder or injury perpetrated by the State—is, by definition, that of clarifying all uncertainties, of dismantling the killers' staging. Who, where, when, how, and why? These questions must be asked and answered as clearly and precisely as possible. One must do this in spite of the disinformation traps, the destruction of evidence, the physical threats, and the lies told by the architects and perpetrators of the violence. In such an endeavor, uncertainty is an enemy to be defeated.

But what about investigating in the other direction and interviewing a person who has survived State violence? One supposes that such a person's testimony would be the fundamental element for clarifying the uncertainty, that such testimony would be precisely what the "freedom of expression of the killers" seeks to erase, destroy, ridicule, or annihilate. So, when facing such a testimony, should all uncertainty be seen as an enemy to defeat? Should one allow, out of respect for the testifying person's pain, the omission of certain information? How does that which goes unsaid affect the trust one places in the testimony?

A person's decision to not tell everything presents the writer with a dilemma. This dilemma, for me, is not one of whether or not to continue with the writing, nor much less to try to convince the person who survived the violence to tell it all. The dilemma is something other. It is a methodological, and hence, philosophical dilemma. It is not a matter of responding yes or no, but of asking how.

The British poet John Keats mentioned, just once in a

letter, a concept he called "negative capability." He defined it this way: "When a [person] is capable of being in uncertainties, mysteries, doubts, without any irritable reaching after fact and reason." This quality, according to the poet, is necessary for literary work: *to be* amidst uncertainties. To be able to live within and navigate through mysteries. Amongst other things, this is a quality that promotes humility: From the beginning, one must recognize that one does not know and will not know everything. In our present case, the situation is a bit different. Here it is not an issue of deciding between mystery and reason, nor of thinking that they are incompatible. The challenge is how to write within the uncertainties, mysteries, and doubts while seeking out all the information one can find. How to respect and include the silences of the person who lived through the acts of State violence and injury?

Let's consider for a moment the two fields of uncertainty present here: that of the will and that of trauma and memory. The parameters of the uncertainty of the will present here are themselves clear. Tzompaxtle told me directly: "This isn't a dead man's book. This book is about someone alive. The book won't tell the whole story." And by "the whole story" he is speaking of his life after returning to clandestinity and to any and all information that could be used to locate and identify him now. The other field contains two overlapping dimensions: that of trauma and that of memory. The fragility of memory, like that of the body, is something most people experience on a daily basis. Most people have had the experience of remembering in absolute clarity something that never happened. It is quite common. Memory fails; memory leaves traps. That is why we seek verification: we consult other people, check our notebooks, look in the dictionary, or—with increasing frequency and often vexing results—look on the internet. And this is in cases where one's memory is in perfect health. What happens when someone tries to recall events related to profoundly traumatic experiences?

If some wicked being were to develop a procedure to dismantle one's memory, soon they would arrive at the most common practices of torture: blows to the head, provoking the overproduction of stress-related hormones, malnutrition, lack of sleep, depression, physical pain in general. All of these experiences affect memory.[2] How then can one reliably document torture? Torturers usually do not give interviews or publish evidence of their torture sessions. The survivor's testimony is the essential evidence. And here it is necessary and urgent to note that the uncertainty that arises from the failures of memory does not block or damage the truth of the testimony. Survivors tend to make mistakes recalling details regarding date, time, number of people present in certain moments, some specific characteristics (were they police or soldiers?), and details related to the most traumatic experiences, such as torture and rape. But the survivor does not make a mistake about having been tortured or not, having been raped or not. If we needed them, even the studies agree that mistakes do not justify mistrust: "Current research on memory shows that stories can change for many reasons and the changes do not necessarily indicate that the narrator is lying."[3]

Dori Laub writes about the story of a genocide survivor and witness to an uprising in Auschwitz. The witness told, in the midst of a long testimony, how she saw four chimneys explode in flames and people running. Laub describes a conference with historians, psychoanalysts, and artists in which the historians tried to discredit the woman's entire testimony because she had the number of chimneys wrong. Laub responded: "She had come, indeed, to testify, not to the empirical number of the chimneys, but to resistance, to the affirmation of survival, to the breakage of the frame of death."[4]

Nora Strejilevich, a survivor of torture during the military dictatorship in Argentina, proposes that one must understand that the survivor's testimony will always have absences, silences, and contradictions. She writes: "Memories of horror are not accurate, and witnesses who testify in front of a jury have to reshape their traumatic recollections to fit the requirements of the law, which demands precision. A truthful way of giving testimony should allow for disruptive memories, discontinuities, blanks, silences and ambiguities; it should become literary."[5]

The essence of knowledge about torture is different from other forms of knowledge. Its roots lie in the memory of an experience, a trauma that breaks and evades linguistic expression.[6] Torture is an extreme act of rupture and isolation. The impossibility of communicating such pain, and the disconnection from language within the experience of pain—both imposed through the studied and refined cruelty of torture—cut off and isolate the person being tortured. The interrogation, a return to language, is the effort to reunite the tortured person with the torturers through language, but in a position of absolute subordination. The interrogation is an essential element of torture and amplifies the psychological dimension of the horror: They destroy your language, they isolate you from the world only to bring you back to language bound to them in a relation of domination and humiliation. Over and over again.

One of the things that Tzompaxtle most emphasized in his memory of torture was the bludgeoning, incessant repetition of the same questions, and how the only terrain in which he could combat them was precisely that of language.

We are responsible for what we say precisely because our speech represents our will. Torture seeks to violate this representation: It seeks to force a person to say what he or she profoundly does not want to say, and it does this by subjecting the person to excruciating pain. The torturer inflicts and administers such pain while demanding that the person being tortured say what the torturer wants. What is more, the torturer insists that the tortured person is responsible for their own suffering, that the person chooses pain by choosing not to speak. This is the logic of torture, always a brutal mystification of the torture acts and the responsibility for them.

Telling the story of what one suffered under torture, denouncing the torture and the torturers may be, for some, a part of the process of healing, of reclaiming the language brutalized by one's torturers.

How to understand what it means to resist such horror? I don't know. But I think it is important to try to do so, to approach the possibility, to *listen* to Tzompaxtle and other survivors like him, to listen to their stories, to acknowledge what they suffered, what they achieved, and through such acknowledgment to participate in some way in the collective resistance to the persistence of that pain.

THE INTERVIEW

ON APRIL 5, 1997, *LA Jornada* published on the lower right-hand corner of the back page the headline: "EPR fighter was tortured to make him implicate the PRD and two journalists." The article by Rosa Rojas begins:

> EPR guerrilla fighter Andrés Tzompaxtle Tecpile, alias Rafael, was "disappeared" from October 25, 1996, until last February 22. He declares that he was detained by military intelligence agents and tortured physically and psychologically during his capture, which was carried out in secret jails located at the Llano Largo base in Acapulco and then the Teotihuacán Military Camp, in Mexico State, from which he escaped.

The reporter mentions a written testimony "dated April 25" and sent to the newspaper. The article continues on the lower left-hand portion of page 22 and appears next to a black-and-white passport-size photograph of Andrés Tzompaxtle Tecpile. Tzompaxtle is looking ahead. He has a mustache and wears a checkered shirt. He does not smile. The article occupies three columns, contains twenty-four paragraphs and cites Tzompaxtle's written testimony at length. It continues:

> During the torture sessions, "they told me that if I didn't want to make declarations against my organization that they'd give me another opportunity to save myself: I would have to appear publicly saying that Cuauhtémoc Cárdenas supplies us with weapons, that Manuel López Obrador, Ranferi Hernández, and Félix Salgado Macedonio advise us and are behind the EPR. They promised that upon saving my life they'd let me go, give me money, send me to study abroad, and protect my family.
>
> "They told me that revolutionary propaganda is fundamental, similar to realizing a military attack, that armed propaganda hurts them, just like attacking a base.
>
> "They asked me about the reporter from *El Sur*, Maribel Gutiérrez, (what rank she holds in our organization) and they also asked about Juan Angulo (the director of *El Sur*), Rosario Ibarra, and other people who have nothing to do with our organization.
>
> "They showed me some of our communiqués, and about the message to the journalists they said: 'These are well written; they are not written by a laborer or a campesino; this is written by an intellectual. Who? Which journalist or Congressperson is writing your stuff?'"

Tzompaxtle Tecpile, who says he is a 27-year-old Náhuatl [sic] indigenous man from the Zongolica Sierra of Veracruz, says that his captors also asked him about Omar Garibay, about his activities with the POCUP [sic] and about his supposed participation in the OIPUH (Independent Organization of United Pueblos of the Huasteca).

"Once they asked why we didn't negotiate and become a 'peaceful' guerrilla movement, but at another point they said that they'd never negotiate with us, that they feel a boundless hate for the EPR because we are radicals."

In a section titled "The capture," the reporter writes:

Rafael, whom the Army denies having detained, says he was captured in Zumpango del Río, Guerrero—during a unilateral cease-fire declared by the EPR—when he was leading, with other EPR members, a number of journalists toward a camp where they would carry out an interview with EPR's regional command.

And then she again cites the document:

"Military Intelligence (IM) set up a capture operation with at least 25 men, four vehicles, and radio and cellular telephone communications. . . . The IM agents were armed, while we were not armed

due to the peaceful nature of the task we were carrying out, and so as not to put in danger the reporters we were leading to the interview."

In a section titled, "Torture," she again cites the document:

"During the first two months in captivity I was subjected to 30 to 40 sessions of electric shocks applied
all over my body, including my head and genitals;
the frequent placement of plastic bags over my head
to take me to the edge of suffocation; the pouring
of mineral water down my mouth and nose; palm
strikes over my ears; hanging me by the neck to
the point of strangulation; simulations of cutting
my throat, rape, and castration; constant beatings,
amongst other abuses. Even thus, the psychological
torture was the worst, the threats of raping and killing my children (younger than five years of age), my
wife, and my mother.

And then the reporter adds: "The first two months he
had—he said—his feet bound and his hands cuffed behind
him, and he was blindfolded."

In a section titled "The Torturers," she cites the document without preamble:

"The torturers mostly had Mexico City accents;
they were sergeants or of higher rank; I heard refer-
ences to captains, a colonel, and the highest-ranking

official they called *patrón* [boss]; he traveled by helicopter.

"The patrón told me that he'd been dealing with—that is to say, torturing—people like me for twenty years.

"The 'good' torturer told me that the war is more select now; that soon they might have to kill a lot of people; that there will be massacres, but that for the moment they want to trap us selectively; he proposes that I should join an organization and spy for the government.

"The torturers told me, 'We're from the old school; we respected Lucio because he showed his face, but not Genaro.' They talked to me about Fierro Loza and Carmelo Cortés, as if to show how much they know about us, but they actually said a lot that was incorrect.

"One of the torturers told me that he had broken Zambrano's back—Zambrano is an EPR compañero prisoner in Almoloya—and that he was a specialist in breaking spines and that he was going to leave me an invalid for the rest of my life.

"They told me, 'We're going to use our work to make what happened in Oxchuc (Chiapas) happen to you, we'll turn the masses against you.'"

The last section carries the title "The Detention Locations," and again consists mainly in quotations from the document. It reads:

Tzompaxtle Tecpile states that at the Llano Largo military camp in Acapulco they took him to "a school-like construction surrounded by a wire fence. There are some offices in front, and in the back they have the area set up for torture.

"They put me in a room; it was very hot. I think there was a boiler next to the room, due to the noise it made. There were typewriters there. They used cell phones and took me outside to go to the bathroom.

"It was a military base, because I could hear the marching band and helicopters. There were times when they made me go down a staircase with 22 stairs [sic]. I was blindfolded. They have a room set up with a metal table essential for torture; it resembles the medieval torture racks used in the feudal inquisitions."

On January 20 he claims that they took him to Teotihuacán in a Chevrolet Suburban. There "they kept me in a room with a bathroom, with one hand cuffed to a bunk. The cell where they kept me is inside a larger structure, with a pitched corrugated tin roof about 40 meters long. The windows do not have bars. The bathroom has a Persian window. In front of my cell you can see a residential complex."

He escaped from there on February 22: "I walked between the houses, between 20 and 40, it seems like a residential complex surrounded by a wire fence. It seems like there are various storage rooms and a carpentry workshop of some kind. It is a military base.

"Two soldiers walk by and I pretended to do exercise. I'm wearing pants and have my head shaved. They greet me. It is around six in the morning. They had already played the reveille and it was beginning to get light."

On April 9, 1997, *La Jornada* published an article by José Gil Olmos on the upper left-hand corner of the back page. The article's headline reads: "EPR: The Army Reactivated the White Brigade with Acosta Chaparro in Charge." The article, which continues on page 14, consists of three columns and thirteen paragraphs and is accompanied by a photograph of two masked men sitting behind a table and identified as "Commanders Vicente and Oscar." One of the men holds a rifle. The walls behind them are covered with what appears to be paper.

The article says that in a communiqué commemorating the 78th anniversary of Emiliano Zapata's murder, EPR commanders called for the creation of a truth commission and announced their intention to continue a propaganda campaign and revolutionary self-defense in the face of "the strengthening of the [paramilitary] white brigades intensively trained by the Army and the police" as well as their support for the San Andrés Agreements [signed between the EZLN and the Mexican federal government], which consist in "a heartfelt demand and fair national protest."

Gil Olmos then writes:

A long meeting took place in an EPR safe house

located somewhere in the Valley of Mexico. Reporters traveled to the location through multiple contacts, and were instructed to close their eyes during the final segment of the trip. During the meeting, which was staged in a small room whose surfaces were covered with brown paper and doorknobs masked with tape, the EPR leadership said that it fully trusted Andrés Tzompaxtle Tecpile—Rafael—despite the suspicion created by "his incredible" escape from military barracks. The leadership also maintained its willingness for the combatant to directly present his denunciation before civilian human rights organizations.

Accompanied by his wife, the combatant Rafael again shared his testimony of his abduction and four months spent disappeared in various hidden jails. His wife said that she joined the EPR after her husband's capture and said that she held the government responsible for any repression against his family or friends. They both wore military uniforms and had their faces covered from beneath their eyes down, even though Rafael removed the brown cloth covering his face for half an hour without allowing anyone to take photographs.

The following section of the article is titled "Rafael's Incredible Escape." Gil Olmos writes:

The EPR combatant—supported by his wife and military commanders—said that during the four months of his torture they sometimes video-recorded testimonies in which he "simulated collaborating and accepting the claims of his torturers, signing documents that could implicate Cuauhtémoc Cárdenas, Andrés Manuel López Obrador, Rosario Ibarra, Félix Salgado Macedonio, and Ranferi Hernández, but that it was to lessen the beatings, electric shocks, and waterboarding."

Tzompaxtle explained that his escape was aided by his receiving less food and having lost as much as 14 kilos during the prior month of captivity in the military base in Teotihuacán. For that reason his wrists had become thinner, and he was able to remove them from the handcuffs that bound him to the bunk.

"I toyed with the handcuffs, dreaming about slipping out of them, until one day I did so," Rafael said, recalling that day and night he thought of escaping, trying twice through the only window, located in the bathroom of the 40-meter-long structure, before succeeding on February 22.

After discussing Rafael's medical report and denouncing the reappearance of the [paramilitary] White Brigade that operated in the 1970s against the guerrilla movements under the command of general Mario Arturo Acosta Chaparro, the two EPR commanders said that as soon as the combatant made contact with the organization and told them everything that had happened, "he had our complete support even if under the pressures of torture and inhumane treatment he signed documents put before him or made agreements that were recorded."

Commander Oscar, in civilian dress representing the PDPR, with his face covered by a piece of gray cloth, assured that the EPR will accept Rafael with all the rights and obligations he has as a combatant and "offer all the support to the compañero, who is now receiving permanent psychological treatment and sedation" to lessen the emotional impact and the scars of the torture. . . .

He warned that the EPR remains alert to the government's attempts to infiltrate the organization and "uses objectivity, maturity, and sensitivity" to analyze such attempts made through combatants or sympathizers who have been captured. He assured that they have developed "tasks and methods" over the decades to guarantee the prevention and the "failure" of any possible government infiltration.

The article closes with a renewed call to "independent social groups" to create a truth commission "that could take charge of investigating cases of forced disappearance, torture, incarceration, murder, and massacres over the last thirty years of armed struggle."

That same day, April 9, *El Universal* published a photograph in the lower right-hand corner of the front page showing three people in military uniform, armed, their faces covered with cloth. The photograph, taken by Claudia Fernández, is accompanied by the following caption:

"In a clandestine interview, EPR members conduct a review; they denied any connections with drug trafficking and called for the formation of a truth commission."

On page 18 there are two articles and one photograph by Claudia Fernández. The photograph shows a man in military uniform, his face covered with a bandanna, showing his hands to the camera. The photo's caption reads: "Rafael shows some of the scars left after four months of being tortured by presumed paramilitaries." The first article, with the headline "The government has not been able to strike us: EPR," describes the conditions in which the interview with Rafael took place and coincides with the information published the same day by *La Jornada*. It begins like this:

> The Popular Revolutionary Army (EPR) and the Popular Democratic Revolutionary Party (PDPR) warned of a resurgence of Mexico's Dirty War at the hands of a paramilitary group "under the command of the federal Army and advisors from the United States."
>
> This resurgence has come about through abductions, disappearances, and torture not only of members of the insurgency, but also in the worst ways against social activists and citizen opponents, claimed the EPR commanders Óscar and Vicente.
>
> Likewise, they said that the testimonies of their own combatants, those who have been able to survive abductions and torture, reveal the existence of hidden prisons in the country.
>
> Attempts to confirm this information with the National Defense Secretary were unsuccessful.

During the five-hour-plus interview in an EPR safe house in the Valley of Mexico, Commanders Óscar and Vicente also denied any contacts between the EPR and drug traffickers.

Fernández describes the room where the interview was held and the uniforms and weapons of the EPR militants. She paraphrases and quotes the combatants declaring that the government has not been able to hit them. Then she takes up Tzompaxtle's story, mentioning the place and date of his abduction. She writes:

> Subjected to constant torture for four months, Rafael—whose real name is Andrés Tzompaxtle Tecpile, originally from Veracruz—was held captive in Llano Largo, Acapulco, and then at the San Juan Teotihuacán base from which he escaped last February 22.
>
> His via crucis began with a cold warning from his tormentors: "We feel an incalculable hatred for you and here you are going to pay for everything the EPR has done and will do," Rafael recalled as night fell on Monday.
>
> And this is how it happened: electric shocks all over the body, blindfolded and wet, rape simulations with an iguana's tail, simulations of castration, breaking his back, cutting off his head . . . until his torturers made him suffer a thousand deaths and he began to speak.

Also on April 9, *El Sol de Acapulco* published an article

on the front page with the headline: "Even at the edge of death, the combatant Rafael did not give away anyone from the EPR." The article, by Javier Trujillo Juárez, appears with a photograph showing the journalist taking notes in front of a television screen on which one can vaguely make out two masked people facing a camera. The article, with the subheadline "He endured four months of torture," opens with these lines:

> "You know the life that waits for you. You don't even know that you've come to die here." That was the sentence the combatant Rafael, named Andrés Tzompaxtle Tecpile, received from his torturers.
>
> Speaking to a video camera at a press conference, the insurgent narrates how he was captured and disappeared for four months in different regions of Guerrero, and held at the Military Zone 37 base located in the archaeological zone of Teotihuacán, from which he escaped on February 22, 1997, around six in the morning.

The article continues on page A2, taking up three columns and giving a detailed summary of the recorded testimony. Juárez writes:

> After five days of intense interrogations and savage torture, "almost at the edge of death, I give them my name, Andrés Tzopaxtle [sic] Tecpile, from the municipality of Atozique [sic], Veracruz—in the Zongolica Sierra—to see if that way they wouldn't kill me. They confirmed the information and then

came back to tell me, 'Your family says we should kill you, that you don't matter to them.' 'Okay, I assume my responsibility,' I answered."

The next section of the article carried the subhead, "The doubt . . . the conviction." The reporter writes:

Back in Acapulco, at the police mini-station at the Y intersection known as La Laja, there was a major operation—they had found a safe house—in which more than forty agents participated, raiding houses, going through stores, and conducting surveillance from their cars. They detained a number of people.

"Are these them?" the torturers asked Rafael.

"No," he replied, now without the blindfold covering his eyes.

"They say they are," they told him.

"They aren't, but if they say they are, that's their problem. Because they aren't." He adds: "The men being held identified themselves and said where they lived, and they were the neighbors of where the compañeros rented a place."

It was on November 11 that the torturers— that is how he identifies them throughout almost the whole interview—tell him that they know he is Rafael. "Your compañeros are looking for you."

And they sentenced him: "Here there is no other judge besides us. God, for us, does not exist here."

"At that moment I accepted my death," says the EPR combatant, sitting between his wife and five other masked people, two of whom remain at all times in military position, each uniformed and with an MP-5 7.62 caliber rifle and automatic pistol, apparently a nine millimeter, holstered to their waists. He explains that at that moment he felt the firm determination to "not give anything" to the torturers.

The following day, April 10, *El Sol de Acapulco* published an article on the front page with the headline: "Social activists are not tortured, assures Aguirre R." The article, by María Antonia Cárcamo, the paper's Chilpancingo-based correspondent, reports that Governor Ángel Aguirre Rivero "denied that hidden prisons operate in the state where social activists are tortured." The article continues on page A4, where the reporter cites the governor saying that "it is absolutely false, absurd, it is irresponsible information and I don't know who started spreading it."

Cárcamo then asks him: "But wouldn't it be worth investigating?"

And the governor responds: "How can we investigate something that is totally invented? It is a worthless situation."

I interviewed José Gil Olmos, now a reporter for *Proceso* magazine, in Mexico City. I asked him if he could tell me a bit about what he remembers of attending the interview in April 1997 with Rafael and other EPR members. He told me this:

I don't know if it had been a few months or weeks since he had escaped from a secret prison that I

don't know if the Army still uses near San Juan Teotihuacán. I think that was the name of the place.
Near the pyramids.

I had heard about the story through a testimony that was published somewhere. And, honestly,
it seemed unlikely to me the way that, well, he described how they held him captive, how they had
grabbed him, beaten him, tortured him in a house
and then at some point the soldiers guarding him
left, got careless. He started removing some glass
panes there, some windowpanes that were remov-
able. He took several out of what was like a louver
window in the bathroom, and that was how he got
out. He also told about the handcuffs that they had
used to chain him. If I remember correctly, he said
that he was able to slip out of the handcuffs using
his own blood I think, or something like that. He
was able to take off the handcuffs and then remove
the windowpanes and escape.

After Rafael's testimony was published, I was
invited to an interview with the EPR leadership
at a safe house they have somewhere here in the
Valley of Mexico. The meeting place was here in
the Federal District. They give you a password
and a response and then they send you off for
hours in public transit and taxis all over the city
until you meet the last contact, after which they
have you get in a vehicle and ask you to close your
eyes. They don't blindfold you in case the police
stop them.

And then there's another hours-long trip until

you are taken inside a house that is completely covered with paper: the walls, the floor; even the doorknobs are covered with masking tape.

And, well, there he was. I'm trying to remember . . . Rafael was there, but I think it was Antonio—Antonio or Arturo, one of them—read the EPR's statement about the Mexican State's strategies. They introduced Rafael and denounced what had happened. And then Rafael gives us his testimony again. This is his direct testimony about what he had suffered. I don't remember if it was weeks or months that they had him in a house where they tortured him. They beat him and asked him for information about the EPR commanders. I don't remember specifically if they asked him for information about Arturo and about Antonio, because they were the leaders at the time.

The interview is more a kind of press conference that takes place in a room with nothing in it besides a table where they sit with two flags behind them—one for the EPR and the other for Mexico. Two armed guards are also present, as is a video camera that records everything, which is the EPR's way to be sure that what gets published corresponds to what really happened there.

So it was really . . . he described really well how the Mexican State at that time was carrying out the same kinds of strategies as in the 1970s. These were, in part, illegal detentions, forced disappearances and executions. It was the first testimony—I mean, real testimony at that time—from a member of an armed movement, an insurgent, guerrilla movement, about how he had been abducted.

And this case was emblematic, I think, because it was through this case that we came to know that the Mexican State was carrying out the same strategies that it used during the Dirty War of the 1970s, those things I already described, but also the infiltration of the movements themselves. And through such infiltration, forced disappearances, and torture of the people they took, the State possessed first-hand information.

And Rafael. What I more or less remember about what he said then was that the government had people specialized in this. People who knew exactly what they were doing. But they were not police, but soldiers. So it all seemed to indicate that the Army had developed its own strategic counter-insurgency units. In the 1970s, those who did that were the political police from Gobernación (the Interior Ministry). Now it was the Army itself doing these things. And it used infiltration not only for information, but also to divide the armed movements, provoking mutual accusations amongst the groups.

And that was precisely one of the problems with Rafael's case, because a part of the EPR itself and other groups didn't believe Rafael's version. They said that it wasn't possible to escape in such an easy way. That if it was an Army safe house, surely they would have had it surrounded, guarded. That if they had had him handcuffed, then it would have been practically impossible to remove them. Above all, they didn't believe how he could have left the house so easily.

But that was what Rafael said: Since his captors had him so well handcuffed, they had been confident that nothing could happen. The other thing he said was that as a result of the bad state he was in, he had lost a lot of weight. He had gotten a lot thinner, and that helped him slip out of the handcuffs and escape through the space he had made in the bathroom window.

So his story seems improbable, no? I mean, it didn't appear realistic to some people. Rafael said that the first thing he took on as a responsibility was to appear publicly and give his statement. That way he was showing that he didn't have anything to hide. I think it was Antonio who said that they were appearing with Rafael to demonstrate complete trust and confidence in the testimony of a compañero who continued to be an integral part of the EPR. They did not doubt him. They had no suspicion that he could be an infiltrator now, or that the Army might have let him go so he could be a double agent.

The EPR leadership said that they had investigated Rafael's story, that they had located the safe house, they had found it, and that Rafael's testimony was completely truthful.

José Gil spoke briefly about hidden prisons and then went back to the story of the interview.

So, after the interview/press conference, we didn't hear anything more about Rafael. But what was really proven with all this was that the State was carrying out forced disappearances, that the State had a special intelligence unit for this, and it had all kinds of infrastructure with these kinds of safe houses where they held people captive for extended periods of time. I mean, we're talking about weeks, months, I don't know if years, but . . . Because, beyond proving the existence of these kind of undisclosed detention houses, we don't know what happens to the people who are taken there. There is no information about the people held in these places.

Rafael was thus the clearest and most convincing proof of these strategies of the Mexican State that were thought to have been left behind after most of the insurgent or guerrilla groups had been dismembered in the 1970s and '80s. And then later you saw the EZLN's uprising on January 1, 1994, and in May 1994 with the formation of the EPR, from I think fourteen different organizations. After that, the Mexican State once again takes up the same strategies, the same mechanisms and forms of counterinsurgency.

I think that this is really what happened with Rafael, and that was why it was so important for the EPR to dedicate a press conference specifically to it. Usually, in the EPR press conferences that I went to, their aim was for the commanders to make a statement about something specific. In this case, it was exclusively for us to meet Rafael and hear his story directly from him. It was for that reason, to show Rafael as proof of what was happening.

I asked him what reaction there was to his story.

You know, the story didn't have much of an impact, except in a few media outlets that took it up. *La Jornada*. But others didn't follow the story. I think that during those years when it happened, many of the media outlets were once again bound by government and State authority. So they didn't give these kinds of testimonies sufficient space. Why? Because the denunciation went against the State, against the federal government. And in this case, even more specifically, against the Army. There were already denunciations that the Army maintained secret prisons, but inside military installations. They didn't have safe houses beyond the bases. The safe house in question here is also interesting because it is close to the Santa Lucia air base. It is very, very likely then that the Army has secret prisons near their bases, like the air base here in Mexico State.

This is the other issue, no? To remove suspicions from the EPR itself. Because if we look at the dates, there were already internal differences in the EPR at that time that would finally lead to a split and the creation of the ERPI [Revolutionary Army of the Insurgent Peoples]. They wanted everything to get cleared up. And the media mostly didn't follow the story. The columnists who did follow it,

I don't remember who now, but they pursued the story precisely to create doubts. They said: "No, it is not possible. It isn't possible that he could have escaped." They even commented that a solider was making all this up, as part of a counter-information job. The State very clearly does carry out those kinds of counter-information strategies.

I asked him about the other reporters who were there during the interview. He told me that Claudia Fernández from *El Universal* was there, but that he didn't recall anyone else. Then he told me:

I remember that the interview was delayed for quite a while. They took a long time to begin because, yes, I remember this clearly now: Antonio and Aurora were giving the press conference, if I'm not mistaken. And when Antonio was three or four hours late, they explained to us that they had detected an Army operation. The Army had put a checkpoint in Tepoztlán, on the highway, knowing that the guerrillas would pass by there. So they had to do a series of maneuvers and follow another plan to avoid that checkpoint, and that took several hours.

I remember we asked them about what was going on inside the organization. They said they knew that information about their movements was leaking out. So they had to be very careful.

I remember well that I asked them: "Hey, um, what about us? If there were a military operation and the soldiers were to arrive here, what should we do?" And they just answered us, laughing a bit, "Well, duck."

I spoke with Gloria Arenas Agís in Mexico City. Arenas joined the PROCUP toward the end of the 1980s.[1] In 1996, when Tzompaxtle was disappeared, Arenas held the rank of colonel and participated in the Guerrero state command. Around the end of 1997 and early 1998, the majority of EPR guerrillas in Guerrero state left that organization and founded the Revolutionary Army of the Insurgent Peoples (Ejército Revolucionario del Pueblo Insurgente, ERPI). In October 1999, Arenas was abducted, disappeared for several days, tortured, and then arrested and jailed. After a ten-year legal battle she waged with her compañero Jacobo Silva Nogales—Guerrero state commander of the EPR and later co-founder of the ERPI, who was also disappeared, tortured, and jailed in October 1999—Arenas achieved her freedom. She now studies, writes poetry, and participates in social movements.

About Tzompaxtle's case, she told me this: "I don't know if Rafa escaped or not. It is possible, and I lean toward believing that it's true. But that is not important. For me what matters the most is what he did afterward: He did not betray us. He did not reveal the identities of guerrilla fighters. That I know."

She told me that during the guerrilla struggles of the 1990s it was common for combatants, while being tortured, to falsely agree to be a double agent for the Army so that they could save themselves from the torment and disappearance. "Some people got out that way," she told me, "otherwise they would be dead now. It is completely valid.

What matters is what they do after they get out: They came and told us frankly what had happened."

Tzompaxtle's case was similar, she said. After leaving the Army base, he sought contact with the organization and then continued participating, and the people he knew were never detained or disappeared.

"He didn't turn over the house, for example," she said. "He knew people, knew where they lived, where their rooms were located. Those people never fell. During an Army operation he recognized some compañeros and didn't signal them. And it wasn't a short while. It was a long time that he was disappeared. That tells you something."

I asked her about the house in Acapulco. "A group went to remove everything from the house," she told me:

> But they did a bad job of it. I don't recall, but perhaps it was a month after his disappearance. The group went to take everything out of the house and make sure it wasn't being staked out. Do people want proof? That is proof: The house was not under government watch. The compas went and they made a mistake. They took out some appliances, but they left the things that showed that it was a guerrilla house. It wouldn't have mattered if they had left a camera, a television, or a bicycle. Even though I understand what they were going through. I didn't go on that mission, for example, and did not have to face all the fear and nervousness that it would have involved.

Some time passed, and the EPR members in Guerrero

were surprised when they saw the news about the house, the police, and the Army operation in Acapulco. "I found out later through others that when the house was found, Tzompaxtle went through some of the hardest times. It was the organization's mistake. But he paid the price, and it must have cost him quite a lot. But even after that mistake, his attitude was admirable, I think. Even though he did have an understandable critique, he didn't turn out resentful or become a traitor."

That critique was one of the points of discord between Tzompaxtle and his commanders. "Those of us in the Guerrero state command structure didn't care so much about probing all the particulars. That was not important to us. At that time the government was killing and capturing compañeros in Guerrero, and *that* was what mattered to us: what Tzompaxtle did afterward. Because not a single compañero fell due to him."

A PIECE OF BEING

A SOLDIER SHOUTS, "HEY!" BUT then he doesn't do anything, as if this happens every day, a common routine whereby neighbors cut through the military sports fields, just one more annoyance. But you walk without looking back, with your hands up, behind your head, a gesture somewhere between fear and trying to look like you're stretching, out for a morning run. And with every step, every breath, you wait for the gunshot. The end. You chose this and here it is. It is as if you were already hearing the sound of the explosion that will knock you to the ground, dead. As if sounds carried shadows that could fall forward in time, an echo that precedes its sound. It is as if you could already hear it, feel the burn of the bullet before it penetrates the skin. As if death were already walking beside you. You feel it close. You wait for it with every step.

But it doesn't come. *In this lapse of time your emotions swell, your veins dilate, and you keep going, you continue walking.* You think, *I will not go back.* Another internal voice wants to prepare you for being recaptured: *Well, and if I tell them that I made a mistake . . .* But you snap out of it in an instant: *No, fuck that! This is combat.* You grab the back of your head waiting for the shot. You've walked about eighty meters, and the shot that comes is inside you: Now you have to defecate. Now. The adrenaline reproduces the effect of the electrical shocks. You know how to recognize unstoppable powers, and this is one of them. Either you find someplace behind a tree or bush, or you'll shit your pants. You go behind some short shrubs and try to squat, but your legs are too weak and you fall. After you pull out some thorns, defecate, and clean yourself with leaves, you keep walking.

You come upon a man who has taken his sheep out to pasture. You approach. You pretend to be drunk and say:

"Where am I? I don't . . . I drank last night . . . Where am I?"

"You're in Teotihuacán."

"And the shared taxis to Mexico City?"

"They pass by here, but on the other side."

"Ah, okay."

You walk toward the street without looking back. With every step you think: *Surely they've realized by now.* A collective taxi drives by. You stop it and ask the driver:

"How much do you charge to Mexico City?"

"I'm not going into the city, those cars pass on the other side of the road. I'm just getting back."

You get back off about a hundred meters down the road. A hundred meters farther away. You can't travel on the highway, you think. At any moment they will notify the police and start setting up checkpoints. You walk into the neighborhood by the road without knowing where you are going, but moving away from the road and away from the base. You have lost more than thirty pounds. You're skeletal, skin sucked to the bone. Your face has aged as if they had torn your youth off you like flesh. Your laceless shoes look like pieces of some thick cloth wrapped around your feet. Your clothes—the same clothes you wore the day they abducted you four months ago—are little more than rags. They were never washed, only rinsed the few times you bathed with your clothes on. Your beard is months long. Your hair, which they would cut randomly with scissors, tells, as does your entire appearance, that you are not walking out to greet the day from a normal situation.

You see another man walking and you approach him. You tell him that you were kidnapped in Mexico City, that you were beaten. You tell him that your captors threatened to accuse you of crimes you didn't commit. You say that you don't have any money to get home and that you are afraid they will find you again and kill you. *I'm lost, I don't have anything. They are looking for me and they want to hurt me.* You ask the man to help you with some old clothes, that you can pay him by doing some work. He tells you that his house is far. He looks at you from head to toe. Then he takes off his old, half-torn jacket and gives it to you. You thank him and ask him that if anyone asks about you to say that he hasn't seen you. He says don't worry, he won't say anything. You put on the jacket. It disguises you a little. Very little.

You keep walking and asking people to help you with a little change for the collective taxi fare. Two women give you four pesos. You wait next to a large truck hoping that the driver will return and give you a ride. But the driver doesn't appear and you get nervous standing there. You walk up to a collective taxi station. You ask one of the drivers if he can take you a bit down the road. You tell him that you don't have any money. He looks at you, annoyed, perhaps suspicious, and tells you that he's waiting for more passengers to arrive before leaving. You wait. When two people arrive the driver tells you, "Get in." After about twenty minutes on the road, the driver gives you two pesos and fifty cents and points out the collective taxis that go to the next town.

You walk up to one of the vans and ask the driver how much the fare is. He tells you, somewhat aggressively, seven pesos. You don't have enough. You walk away and head into the town until you see a construction worker on a street corner. You walk up, say hello, and ask him for work. You tell him that you were robbed and beaten and that you need money to get back to Mexico City. He asks you to help him mix some concrete and you earn five pesos. In a corner store you buy a soda, a piece of bread and some cookies. You walk to a tree next to an empty field to eat, rest, and think. It must be about eleven in the morning. Several hours have passed since you jumped over the fence at the edge of the Army base. You cannot travel to Mexico City on the highway now, and you haven't had the best of luck with rides. You don't trust the roads. *If only there were dark, underground roads.*

You walk toward some bushes that you see in the distance. You cross some train tracks and follow a path. After a bit you turn and see a Ford pickup truck with a camper and a van similar to those used by the Army for their secret ops. Both vehicles advance slowly along a dirt road. They're following you. You try to hide behind a small tree. There is nowhere to run. You wait. The truck and van pass by about sixty meters away and keep going until they reach a paved road up ahead. They take the paved road and drive off. At that moment you hear an airplane overhead. You look to the sky and see a military plane circling. They must be looking for you. They must have found some of the people you asked for help and followed you.

You stop, then cross the road and walk toward a group of houses. First it was those strange vehicles and then the plane. They're launching their operation, that is what you think as you walk toward the houses. *This is the race against everything. The greater the distance, the better. The more miles you put between you and the Army base, the better.* You see a man in front of his house. You tell him that you were mugged in the city, that your captors beat you and made you confess to crimes you didn't commit and then finally threw you out of a vehicle near Teotihuacán. You tell him that you are ashamed to be wearing clothes that are so dirty and torn. You ask him if he could help you out with a bit of old clothes, perhaps let you rest for a bit in his house, that you are terrified that the men will grab you again. The man tells you that it sounds like you've had a rough time, but that you can't stay in his house. He gives you a threadbare old cap and wishes you luck. You thank him and keep going. *Every step, a step toward hope, the hope of having walked a hundred meters.*

At another house you repeat the same story and ask for permission to rest for a bit. An elderly couple making handicrafts with plaster listens to you. You offer to help them, but they say no. The man adds that their son is a detective with the police station in Teotihuacán and might be upset to see the likes of you when he gets home. Just what you needed: to ask for help at a cop's house.

You keep walking, *a piece of being roaming the streets, undone. This is not some guy who jumps a fence and then runs off. No. Every step he takes is a hope of life and a risk of death. Here he does not know who he is, he does not know where he is going. He simply walks, walks, walks . . . You could jump over the edge of hell right here and three blocks down the road come upon something worse. You will find the end. That's why you can't get excited. You have to take it in stride. You walk as far as you can.*

You come to another small town, but decide to avoid the center. Amidst some magueys you find some bushes and sit down there to rest a bit. You look up to where the airplane keeps circling. It is, without a doubt, a military plane.

You walk again. In the distance you see a man collecting sap from the magueys. You approach and tell him that you are a bit lost. You ask him for the names of the surrounding towns and for the way back to the highway. He tells you the names of the towns and points out the path to the highway. You keep going, now with more information, and you realize that the plane is making increasingly wide circles, as if it were searching for you. But then, as you look at the plane more closely, you see that paratroopers are jumping out at intervals, as if they were creating a siege, a half-circle precisely in the direction you are walking.

You watch how they descend, so certain, one after the other, hanging in the air as if the sky had begun to sweat. After so many coincidences—the soldier who instead of shooting you greeted you in the predawn morning, the neighbors you saw going through the hole in the fence, the man who gave you a jacket, those who had given you a few pesos, a cap—to see the paratroopers in the sky feels like being taunted: the sky's own arrogance. It is as if the horizon were repeating what your torturers told you so many times: "*This is the face and the true power of the State.*"

Yes it scares you. You look down the path and see nothing but magueys and bushes between you and the siege floating down from the sky. Half a mile away? A mile? You don't know how far away they are. You don't know if others have already descended before you realized what was happening. You don't know how many they are, or what kinds of weapons they carry. You only know that there is no going back. Not for you. You can't turn around. Going back would be like giving up. You have already looked too closely into the end to doubt yourself. You keep going. You can make them shoot you. You can wait for them to recognize you and attack. You can take one of them with you.

You think, again, that you will see your death in only a matter of moments. Even if there is a remote possibility that you'll find a hole in their siege, a way out. *In that hole you can burn, be destroyed, be broken. But that doesn't matter, what matters is that you are ready for the test.* Moreover, you are not escaping. *You choose your own end. That end is death, and before death there are no obstacles. By declaring yourself dead, there are no more barriers.* You walk with rocks in your hands. "There are things that can only be done with death stepping on your heels."[1]

But you don't come upon any soldiers, or anyone else. You walk to the next little town. You do not know that the paratroopers are not after you. You don't know that the Santa Lucia Airbase is also close by and that the most likely thing is that the terror curtain you saw in the sky was really a routine military exercise. But just the same, you found that hole. The soldiers were all too real. How did you do it? Was it luck? It is better not to seek some speculative answer that could explain everything. Where reason cannot reach, it is better not to dislocate it to force some false explanation. It is better to get used to navigating through the uncertain. There is something more important than explanations here: Having decided to die, you keep walking in order to subvert that ruthless desire for power of those who cultivate others' pain, of those who have experimented with your pain for four months. *Why does everything have to happen at the same time? If we were a bit superstitious, we'd say, well, that you are being tested.*

Yes, you are *a piece of being roaming the streets, undone*, but you are also a warrior. Not like the Special Forces soldiers in the Hollywood films who escape from certain death with their infinite knowledge, their rigorous training in the tactics of war, and their sudden ability to construct an impenetrable fortress in a forest with a pocket knife. Nor like the very real Special Forces troops trained in the U.S. School of the Americas or the Kaibil training center in Guatemala to torture without leaving scars. No. For you to be a warrior is not something learned in a school. It is not a matter of technical knowledge, nor doing to others what has been done to you. Being a warrior comes from your roots in a culture denied though never destroyed. It comes from the commitment to continue being, as a person and as a people, to survive. For you, being a warrior is a spiritual path.

You keep walking. *You do not think that you have won yet.* You come upon an unpaved road that leads to the next town and you take it. On the road you see two shepherds with their sheep and you walk up to chat with them. You walk with them into the town, and through the center. They give you directions to a store with a pay phone, but you find it closed. You have bad luck with phones. You go to a tortilla shop and buy a peso's worth of tortillas and ask for a pinch of salt. There is a butcher's shop across the street. You greet the owner and tell him that you don't have enough money to pay for a collective taxi to the next town. Could he help you out? He thinks about it. He looks you over and gives you four pesos. You thank him and walk away. Up ahead you ask for directions to the path—not the road—that leads to the next small town, and a man points out the way.

You see an old man planting magueys. You sit down nearby to rest for a bit. The journey, some eight or nine hours long by now, takes its toll on you. Everything—the sun, the hours, the fear, the tension, and all the pain— weighs you down at the same time that you feel your freed body come back to life. *You don't realize that you were more dead than alive and that you are now facing the fear of revival. You are coming back to life, and that is a whole new problem because now everything hits you.*

The man looks you over suspiciously. He tells you that there has been a lot of livestock and crop theft lately. That the thieves aren't from around here. He tells you that about two weeks ago the locals killed two such thieves and that it would be best for you to watch yourself lest you be confused with such a thief. You tell him that you look so beaten and messed up because you yourself were mugged and that you prefer to walk and ask for help than steal from anyone. With that little chat your rest comes to an end.

You walk for an hour and a half and come to the edge of another little town near a highway. At the first house you pass you shout a greeting, and a kind-looking woman comes out, smiling. You say hello and ask for her husband, you say you are looking for work. The woman tells you that her husband has left for work and won't be back until nightfall. You ask her for a glass of water and she gives you two glasses of hibiscus tea. She recommends you ask farther down the road, perhaps someone will have some work that needs doing. You walk a few blocks and then see a small corner store. You go inside. You ask for a razor and ask how much it costs. "Four pesos," the young clerk at the store tells you. You have exactly four pesos. You pay the clerk and ask if he could give you a bit of water to shave. He takes you a bucket of water and some soap.

"*I don't have any more money to pay for the soap.*"

"*It's enough paying for the razor.*"

You go outside, where you saw a mirror, to shave. *This also hits you: For the first time, you see yourself in a mirror and you find that you are not yourself. You never would have wished for this. This is a hard thing to see. You never would have done this to yourself, nor allowed anyone else to do it to you. It takes you a moment to shake these feelings. Yes, they strip you of your identity, they tear out who you are, and they know it.*

The young man stands near you and you tell him that you were kidnapped and beaten. You tell him that you were left in the middle of nowhere and are now walking penniless, ashamed of your appearance, and very afraid of running into your tormentors again. You ask him if he could help you, let you rest here until dark.

He tells you that he doesn't know anything about

kidnappings but that it "sounds fucked up." He tells you that there is a military base about fifteen minutes away from here. One time, he says, he and a friend were watching the soldiers do some exercises from the other side of a fence and they laughed when one of the soldiers tripped and fell. The soldiers trapped them and beat the crap out of them. When the soldiers finally let the clerk and his friend go, they said they would kill the two of them if they told anyone about the beating.

"*I don't know, man,*" he tells you, "*but those guys are assholes. They'd fuck over anyone. I don't know if what you're telling me is true, but what you describe, the soldiers have done that to a bunch of people.*"

He tells you that he can't help you out with any money, but that maybe the owner of the store could help.

You tell him that perhaps it would be better not to draw the attention of the owner. You tell him you are really afraid. But the clerk says that the owner is a good guy, and he calls for him. After a bit the owner comes outside. You tell him a bit of what you told the clerk and ask for help. The man asks why you don't have any wounds on your face, why it doesn't seem like you were just beat up. He thinks you want to deceive him, sleep for a while in his house only to rob him in the night. You start to get nervous about standing still, talking for too long there next to the store, near the highway, in plain sight. You are looking for *some kind of refuge*.

"Okay," you tell him, "If you don't want to help me, that is your right. I'm a stranger. But if anyone asks you whether you've seen me, please tell them no. I would very much appreciate that. Rest assured that I am no criminal and that I have spoken honestly."

"Look," the owner says, "I'll take you over to where some fellows are working on a small construction site. Perhaps they can help you out with a bit of work."

The two of you walk toward the outskirts of the town, climb a hill, and from the top of the hill look out to where some people are building a small chapel some thirty meters from where you stand. The man whistles to the workers. One of them waves for the two of you to approach. As you walk up to the chapel you see four men, one of whom had walked by when you were talking to the man and the clerk in front of the store.

You greet them and once again tell the story that you have been making up over the course of the day. The men seem suspicious but also kind. Looking at you they can tell you've been through something hard, even if they don't know what. They ask you if you're involved with drugs. You say that if you were a narco you'd call your gang rather than walk through the brush from town to town asking for help. You can see them doubting you and you add that the men who abducted you know how to wound and kill without leaving evidence in their wake. The men nod in agreement.

One reaches for change in his pocket. The others then do the same and they pull together about twenty-five pesos: "We'll give you this money so you can go buy something to eat. But don't go into our town, go make your purchases in the town over on the other side and then come back and sleep here in the chapel. If someone sees you, don't tell them we've helped you. And don't go telling more people about what happened to you, it puts you at risk. If someone asks, say you got drunk and got lost. Tomorrow we'll bring you something to eat and see if we can help you with anything else. If you're not here when we return, then we'll know you were lying to us."

One of the men takes off his sweater and hands it to you so you don't get too cold at night. Another tells you: "*You'll be fine here. No one will come looking for you, nobody comes around here. Stay inside the chapel and we'll see you tomorrow.*"

After that they all head off toward their homes. You walk to the small town they mentioned and buy some bread, cheese, and a bit of ham. It gets dark as you walk back to the chapel and you lose your way. You decide to look for a place to spend the night. You find a kind of hollow between some rocks and behind some thorny bushes. You climb in and sit with your back to the rocks and try to sleep. Soon the temperature drops and you can't fall asleep.

After long hours with your body numb from the cold you hear someone whistle, then some dogs barking, and then voices. The thought is inevitable and immediate: *They found me*. With those dogs surely they will find you in a matter of moments. You hide farther back amongst the rocks and think: *They'll have to kill me to get me out of here.* If they find you now then all the effort, all the past hours of walking along the edge of the impossible, it will all be in vain. How to defend yourself? How to escape again? You take stock of your possessions and your surroundings: some bread, cheese and a soda, cold, fear, and darkness. Your body, like your clothes, is ragged. You don't have much room to maneuver in your nook between the rocks. The only thing you have going for you is the implacable will to not be disappeared again.

One possibility would be to snap, for your neurons to burst right there and go crazy, lose all of reason. The other possibility would be to wait until the very last second. What do you need, then? A kind of coldness? Perhaps. Yes, always keep fighting. You think: *I will never be prepared to lose. I will fight up until the very last thing I can do. What is that last thing? Who knows?*

This keeps you from running, from screaming, from surrendering, even though you know you're trembling and losing a shred of life.

The men approach your nook. You can see the light from their lantern and one of the dogs comes close, barking intensely. You hear the voice of the dog's owner calling it. "That is not a cop," you think. They must be hunters. But still, how do you explain to an armed man from this area why you are out in the cold hiding in the rocks and bushes? If this man comes upon you, he'll shoot, or the dog will attack. The hunters will overpower you and then you could end up back with them. All day skirting death just to make a stupid mistake . . . But no, the hunter does not come close to where you are hiding. He keeps calling the dog until finally the dog goes back to him. You hear them move away bit by bit. You breathe in and once again feel the pains in your body and the cold.

You endure until dawn. You come out of the hollow and move about, stretching your muscles. Sometime around nine in the morning you find the path back to the chapel. You see more people there than the previous afternoon. You also see a large truck with dirt. They are leveling the floor. You greet two of the men who helped you, pick up a shovel and start working with them. You make note of how they talk and joke amongst themselves as they work. *They show you what life is. There is joy here.* You learn that they are building the chapel with money that migrants from the community working in the United States have sent back. Several of those migrants have returned to help with the construction. You listen to their tales of migrant life in the U.S., and also the stories from life in the town, soccer games and fights with referees. All their joking around makes you feel safer with them. *It is joyful fucking around, not derision or mockery. It is that kind of fucking around that eases your depression. It is a reflection, a manner of expressing the spirit of the community.*

The truck makes two trips. With all the people helping, the floor is soon level. A car with two people in it pulls up and they start to hand out meals, pulque, and sodas. One of them comes up to you and tells you to eat your fill.

After eating they leave. You stay sitting there and the men you had already spoken with approach and ask you what you've thought about doing. You tell them about the scare you had last night and they tell you not to worry: Those were hunters out looking for rabbits at night. Then you ask them if they could help you out with some clothes and a ride out of the area. They say that they know a bus driver who goes to Mexico City and could put you in the luggage area. That sounds risky to you, not because you mistrust them, but if the police have a checkpoint on the highway, they could find you. You ask if there might be another option, someone heading to a different state. They tell you they will ask around and come back in the afternoon with an answer and some food.

You wait. The afternoon hour when they were

supposed to come back arrives, but they do not. After another hour you decide to return to the spot where you weren't able to sleep last night. Tomorrow you'll look for a path to keep going. You eat what's left of the bread and cheese. You climb back in the hollow, back against the rocks and wait for the exhaustion in your body to defeat the cold and let you sleep.

For the moment you don't think about all you've been through. The scenes of your torture don't come to mind. *There is no room to repeat that. You need to go, go. At every moment the idea is escape, escape, escape. During this escape you can feel blows, strikes, whatever. As long as they don't kill you. You want to get away. You think that you are fleeing and being chased. There is no time for looking back.* Nor do you think of the future, of seeing your compañera or your children. No. Since you said goodbye to them that evening in Zumpango del Río you keep them protected, in a safe place. It is still not time to return to them.

Where were you going? Suppose they find you. Where were you going? Who were you going to see? And so you respond automatically: "I wasn't going anywhere." Who were you going to see? No one. I was looking for work anywhere I could find it. This is combat. Focus on this and nothing else. Do what you must. Don't think beyond the necessities of the moment.

In the morning you walk back into the town where you bought food the other evening. With the little change you have left you buy some food and look for a phone. Someone gives you directions to a store with a pay phone, but you find it closed. If you're lucky the store might open by eleven in the morning, but you don't want to wait in the town that long. It seems too risky.

Despite the risks, you return to the town of the men who helped you. You'll ask for help once again and look for a phone. Then you'll be on your way. You can't stay here any longer.

You pass near the chapel and see a man riding a burro. You start to veer a bit so as not to walk by him, but you hear someone whistle and see that the man is waving for you to go over to him. A bit afraid, you walk toward him and as you get closer you see that it is the store owner who took you to the chapel on the first day.

Without getting off his burro, he hands you two tamales and a cup of atole. He had come looking for you, to see if you'd gone yet. In the town the rumor is already going around that a strange man is sleeping in the chapel, and this is putting people at risk. You tell him that you had been waiting for the men to return yesterday until late. But he tells you that it would be best if you found another route that didn't go through this town. He asks you where you want to go. Veracruz, you tell him. He thinks for a bit and then tells you to hurry up with your meal so you can give him the cup back. You finish the atole and hand him the cup. Somewhat hesitant, he tells you that he might know somebody heading in that direction who could give you a ride. But he's afraid that perhaps you're lying so that you can steal someone's car on the journey. You ask him to please let you speak with the person going toward Veracruz. Very cautiously he tells you: "Look, I'll go speak with him and see if he agrees to meet with you. Wait for us here until three in the afternoon. If we don't come by that time, leave. If you stay here any longer you'll be putting us at risk." You thank him for his help and he leaves.

You stay close by, half hidden amidst some bushes. And again the military planes. You move. Again the trucks. You walk up a hillside. Again the men with rifles. It would seem as if persecution itself had materialized from sky and soil, from nowhere, like humidity. But the planes fly off. The trucks drive by. The men fire a few shots and walk around the hill. As they get a bit closer you can see they carry a dead rabbit.

No one arrives at three. You climb up a boulder and wait a bit more. As dusk begins you hear someone whistle. You walk toward the sounds and see three men and a pickup truck. You draw closer, rounding near them, suspicious, but when they see you they wave for you. You walk up to them and say hello. They ask about your strange maneuvers and you tell them that you got scared again by some hunters and that you're still freaked out from your abduction.

The driver immediately begins questioning you: "If you haven't done anything wrong, why are you afraid to be seen? Why don't you go to the police to file a complaint? Why do you think they'll kidnap you?"

And so once again you tell your made-up story that, though invented, is supported by real trauma. You convince him to give you a ride.

It is sometime after midnight. The driver pulls off the road at a truck stop and you ask him for a few pesos to make a phone call. You walk up to a small store where a woman is selling home-cooked food.

"*Do you have a phone?*"
"*Yes.*"

"May I use it?"

"Yes."

"How much do you charge?"

"Four pesos."

You have exactly four pesos.

"May I use it then?"

"Yes."

"Well, would you mind handing me the phone then?"

"It's right behind you."

You turn around and let out a kind of laugh upon seeing the phone hanging there on the wall. You dial a friend's number. It rings and rings before disconnecting. You dial the number again. A sleepy voice answers. You say hello and use the name that they know you by.

"I'm at the bus station and would like to drop by to visit you all. Are you available?"

"Yeah, we're here. Come on over."

"Okay, but, I have a favor to ask. I don't have any money for a cab. . . . Would you mind covering that and I'll pay you back later?"

"Sure. How long will it take you to get here?"

"About half an hour."

You hang up. You walk up to a taxi and ask the driver if he can take you to your friend's neighborhood.

"How much will it be?"

"Twenty pesos," he tells you. You get in as he looks you up and down, taking in your dirty clothes. You look obviously malnourished.

"What line of work are you in?"

"I load eighteen-wheelers," you tell him and then change the subject. You arrive in about twenty minutes.

"*I don't have any change. Give me a second.*"

You get out and go up to knock on the door. No one answers. You don't have any money to go and call again from a pay phone, much less to pay the taxi, the driver of which, just now, is looking at you suspiciously, as if thinking, "What is this beggar doing in a middle-class neighborhood?" You don't have anywhere else to go. You knock again, loud. Someone opens a curtain inside the house and you say, "*Open up, it's me.*"

They throw the keys out to you: "*Come through the gate and we'll hand you the money for the cab through the window.*"

They hand you twenty pesos and you walk back to pay the taxi driver, apologizing: "*They were asleep.*" The driver keeps looking you over, bewildered.

Your friends, a couple, also look you over when you go back through the gate and then close the door. They say: "*If it weren't for your voice we wouldn't have let you in. You don't look like yourself at all.*"

And now you cry for the first time. *Yes, openly weep.*

You tell your friends that you are a guerrilla, that you were disappeared months ago and that you escaped a few days back. Now you are here to ask them for help. If they can't or won't help you, then you only ask that they keep your secret.

"*It's okay,*" the woman says. "*We never knew who you were. Something seemed amiss, but we never thought too much about it. We live a life of comfort. We live in a world different from yours. You live in a world that we don't see. What we can tell you is that, even if you don't say it yourself, we can see that you are just coming out of some kind of hell. You look broken. . . . They tried to destroy you and you resisted. And these are the consequences. But you belong to something you believe in. And precisely what they couldn't do to you was to destroy that spiritual part of you. Don't let that be damaged."*

She doesn't cry with you. Her voice holds strength, almost a kind of scolding, as if she were saying: *You knew what you were getting into, and this result was within the realm of possibilities. You must reckon with what happened to you.*

They make you breakfast. You try to eat but vomit. They tell you: "*Go to sleep.*" But you stay there, sitting in a chair. You can't sleep.

Your friends find you some clothes and you stay with them for two days. You go to a barbershop and they cut your hair. You go back to the house and ask to see a newspaper. You see a story about an EPR communiqué where Commander José Arturo accepts with resignation your disappearance. You see that, and it makes you cry.

You think: "I'm going to try to make contact with them as quickly as possible to tell them that I'm out."

You have to find a contact. You think of a woman with whom you worked before. She knows you. When you see her you ask her to set up a meeting with someone both of you know. In adherence with security protocol, you request that she only tell this person that "a compa" wants to speak with him.

Later she sends word to you of the time and location of the meeting. Two women accompany you on the bus. One of them gets off a few stops before you, the other after you. They are not with the guerrillas, but they move as if they had received guerrilla training.

You see the man as he stares at you. He greets you with a hug, but then freezes. Then he says:

"*What happened?*"

"*I want you to let them know. Tell them I'm out. They didn't let me out: I escaped. I need to tell them what happened.*"

"*When I greeted you I couldn't believe my eyes. All the months you've been gone we held out hope . . . But after so much time disappeared the hope ran out. Just two weeks ago we spoke about you, certain that you wouldn't be coming back, that the chances of you being alive were over. We didn't know anything. Someone told us: 'Surely the compañero is dead.' You didn't send us any signs of life. Two weeks ago we talked about you.*"

Then he tells you: "*In three days I'll let you know what they say.*"

Three days later he sends you a message to go to another town. You say goodbye to your friends and their house forever. You will not go back there. Everything they've done for you . . . all the others that helped you along the way, the men building the chapel, the truck driver . . . all of them. Just thinking about it *makes you commit to protecting them, like a treasure. Everything they did means so, so much.* You think: *I'm alive because of them. Without them this would not have been possible. How can I repay that? There is no payment, no way of . . . The payment is to live, to keep them always in mind, at heart, for the rest of your days. They deserve a tribute for everything they did, for what they are. They probably don't believe in the same things I do, but they are dear, dear human beings.*

Some people pick you up. They take you to a house in a large city. They disguise you clumsily with makeup and a wig. During the drive they treat you with *their characteristic coldness and suspicion.* This is a *cold welcoming.* It is as if they were already telling you: "*We don't believe a word you say.*"

You arrive at the house. What do you think those waiting at the house to see you will do when you arrive? Give you a hug? Show joy, or mistrust? You can't even imagine it. You only know that you must tell them everything.

The commanders for the Valley of Mexico, Óscar and Vicente, arrive. The first interrogations are hard, stemming from distrust: "Whom did you rat out? How much money did you negotiate your release for?"

During this first stage you do not resist. You don't interrupt them, nor debate. Sometimes you can't even talk. Even though that is precisely what you want to do: You want someone to listen to you. But the dynamic here is different. Not only suspicion, which is understandable, but even the rhythm and tone of the interrogation. You start to relive everything . . .

Later the ones charged with studying you arrive, those who will determine whether you tell truth or lies. *They take you to a psychologist and a psychiatrist. They fill you with pills. And the interrogations . . .* You want them to listen to you, but *they turn that into an interrogation. It is as if they had pulled you from that scene and then . . . I mean . . . no, no . . . They take x-rays of* your *whole body, more than thirty x-rays to see if you have a microchip implanted somewhere. Rather than caring about your state of health, they are investigating to make sure you don't "have a tail."*

They tell you: "*You don't have any visible scars. It doesn't look like you've been beaten. We just don't see the evidence.*"

It is so common to say that a torture survivor needs to come out of captivity bleeding, mutilated, dragging pieces of one's

body along the floor. Those people don't understand that tortur-
ers, with all their diabolical, inhuman methodology, have been
perfecting their techniques. These aren't the medieval tortures.
No. In some cases the manner of causing another's pain doesn't
change . . . Today they can wrap you up in a blanket and beat you
with baseball bats without leaving visible scars. They can dislo-
cate your joints and it won't be because they tied you to a horse.

Despite this, you don't feel resentful toward your com-
pañeros. You don't feel hatred. But you know that they do not
understand *the magnitude of the damage done, the martyrdom*
of the body to the human being. They lack that depth of conscience.

Although, *yes, there is a kind of complaint. Why didn't*
they move everything out of the house? Why didn't they trust
me? But this complaint seems like arrogance to them. But you
want them to listen to you; you want to *speak, speak, speak.*
But they criticize everything you say. You are telling your
story and they interrupt you and say: *"No, you're wrong*
there. It doesn't feel like that. It feels this other way." And deep
inside yourself your question to them remains constant:
Have you ever been there? They tell you: *"No, they didn't want*
to kill you. They just wanted to scare you." And you only think:
Oh, you should have told me so earlier, assholes, because I thought
they were going to kill me.

Faced with your comrades' distrust and callousness,
you think: *Now I just want the person who lived through*
something to speak. It shouldn't be hidden. This isn't for me or
for them to interpret. It is just an experience. One experience
amongst many, yes, but this one is mine to tell. Others cannot
tell their stories. Perhaps when they reappear. I didn't do what
I did just to tell, or write, the story. After so much suffering, so
much mistrust, and this denial . . . I don't care. I don't care and

I have no intention of defending myself. Why? Because if it was this or that, or the fight, or something else . . . Fuck it. I have never been that person, nor am I now nor will I ever be. That is not my dream. This is what a rebel must face: either you win or you get screwed in every sense, on every level, with your every move. Okay then, I assume my role as rebel now and always. I identify with that role and not with any other. I don't see it any other way. And I could have never told the story. I could have never said: I am. The one thing that is certain in all this is that I did not fight for an individual, I fought for a different world, for humanity with all that it faces. And this is what happened to me. The fight is against a criminal State, against a State that murders, against a State that massacres, that disappears, that kills. This is hard. I invent, unmake, and take apart my character. Only I can administer the telling of the story so as not to suffer damage. Because to tell the story only to tell it, besides being uncomfortable, is painful. I think that every time I tell the story other things come out, the hidden damage, or the permanence of that hidden damage, or perhaps the healing of it all.

I am not going to force myself to convince you. Perhaps you'll become convinced of something, or a part of it, of one day of it, of nothing, or of everything. I don't know. I simply bear it. That is how I understand it and it is not my role to convince anyone. It is not . . . I am not the one who should be giving explanations. I can do so. Yes. I could answer your absurd questions. I could accept your ridiculous observations, your racist assessment, your arrogance, your delirium in imaging things that don't exist. I could, but no, that also is not a part of my dream.

The EPR commanders decide to organize a press conference to denounce the torture and disappearance you suffered and to publicly support your testimony. First they film you telling your story. They invite some reporters from Mexico City and coordinate so that the videotape with your testimony will be found outside of the local newspapers in Guerrero state on the same day as your interview, so that the news will be published simultaneously in Mexico City and Guerrero.

The reporters arrive. The commanders bring you out in uniform. You tell what you lived through and *the first thing the reporters say is: "The story you're telling is not true." * One of them tells you: *"I just can't believe what you're saying, it seems too elaborate, it seems made up. It doesn't make sense. Why believe everything a combatant says, knowing that he could be a double agent?"*

You don't answer. *The commanders answer: "Look, the dirty war, the death squads in Mexico and the continent, really do use torture in a perverse way to make up stories and destroy human beings. And we, as an army, in another moment, with another combatant, we wouldn't allow the person to reestablish contact with us. We wouldn't be here in this press conference if there weren't something special in this case. And what is special? That the first thing the compañero did upon escaping was to look to reestablish contact with us. He didn't take time trying to hide, suffer, or cry on his own. Instead the first thing he did was look for us. On the other hand, look at the shape he's in. We saw him, the people who see him for the first time detect the state of physical and emotional damage. We even had to keep him on sedatives to calm him down. That is evidence. He is not lying. And lastly, he knows about safe houses, rooms, rearguards, weapons caches, vehicles, and militants, where they travel, what they do and what they don't do. And even when he would have been within his rights to turn any of that over, or some of that information, to avoid the martyrdom and try to save himself, he didn't. Everything is safe. Not one guerrilla has been arrested or pursued. Moreover, in a few places we left some things in case he were to turn them over, so his torturers wouldn't find the places empty. But he didn't turn them over, he didn't even use that resource. That shows his degree of resistance and loyalty. Everything he endured and went through, all of that shows that he deserves to be here. There is no reason to mistrust him because he is telling the truth, he's not making anything up. And not because he says so, but because of everything around him. That's the evidence, everything checks out. And that is the reason that he is here with you all. There is no doubt."*

That was what they told the media, but at the same time, behind closed doors, they don't believe you. They think no, it's not true.

WRITING AND VIOLENCE

ALPHABETIC WRITING THRIVED FOR CENTURIES through the exercise of violence against the spoken word, against song, against other forms of writing, and above all, against those who so spoke, sang, or wrote. This was not the doing of the written word. This was not an inevitable outcome of alphabets, printing technology, ink, or paper. Alphabetic writing and printed books were forced by their early entrepreneurs to become killers.

Notice the difference between an agreement and a contract, between a custom and a law, between generational experience and a property title, between the tales of elders and the National Archive. Power rides with the written word. States structure themselves through texts: constitutions, legislation, codes and laws, newspapers and books, archives and libraries. And the governing classes of those states publicly worship these texts as if they were immortal, until they become inconvenient, in which case the governing classes ignore or rewrite them: Texts do not pull triggers or lock jail cells by themselves. Those who so celebrate such texts generate more texts; they debate, build careers, charge by the hour or by the word, and write an ongoing series of new texts, and then later more texts about the newer generations of texts. Power resides in the domain of the written word and the control over its production.

Linda Tuhiwai Smith writes in her book *Decolonizing Methodologies*:

> Writing or literacy, in a very traditional sense of the word, has been used to determine the breaks between the past and the present, the beginning of history and the development of theory. Writing has been viewed as the mark of a superior civilization and other societies have been judged, by this view, to be incapable of thinking critically and objectively, or having distance from ideas and emotions.[1]

With the creation of the mechanically printed book those who wrote, printed, and read such books called themselves "people of reason" and those who did not "people without reason." This was not merely a matter of arrogance, but a distinction essential to the consolidation of the cruelest institutions of human history: colonialism, genocide, the transatlantic slave trade, patriarchy, and racism. For centuries, European men, with all their reason and printed books, debated in all purported seriousness whether or not non-Europeans were people, whether or not women should be "allowed" to learn to read and write. Those debates, of course, were never about understanding, but about torturing out of reason some way of justifying the unjustifiable, vile treatments of the non-Europeans and the women that those European men developed, institutionalized, industrialized, and got rich off of.

While the printed book became a symbol of power and Europe's proclamation of cultural superiority, both the printing press and paper were first made in China centuries before Johannes Gutenberg printed the Bible in Mainz, Germany, in 1450. As Benedict Anderson points out in his book *Imagined Communities*, printing technology did not have a bigger impact in China because capitalism did not exist there, yet.[2]

"In a rather special sense, the book was the first modern-style mass-produced industrial commodity,"[3] and quite different from the other essential commodities of the young European imperial states and early capitalism, such as sugar, tobacco, and textiles. By 1500, forty-some years after the printing of the Gutenberg Bible, somewhere around 20 million[4] books were printed in Europe. Between 1500 and 1600 the number rose to somewhere between 150 million and 200 million. In his book about the origins of nationalism, Anderson argues that printing technology in combination with the early development of the relations of production known as capitalism, had revolutionary impacts in Europe. Print and capitalism contributed to the fall of Latin as the written language of the elites. They also became an essential part of the Reformation and the success of Martin Luther—"In effect, Luther became the first best-selling author"[5]—and contributed to the consolidation of regional vernaculars such as Spanish and English. (Shortly after the mass printing of books in such languages, the languages stopped the processes of transformation they had undergone before printing: One can read with little difficulty books written in the 16th century, but not those written in the 11th century). And through all this, print and capitalism contributed to the capacity to imagine secular communities defined by those languages and territorial boundaries, the process that would lead to the development of the concepts of nation and nationalism.[6]

In "the Americas," European languages, alphabetic writing, printing, and books all have a bloody history: "Access to written texts in Spanish or Latin was in itself a mark of distinction that separated colonizer from colonized, rulers from ruled, European from native."[7] The prohibition was quite intentional. The Spaniards systematically destroyed Mayan and Náhuatl texts. Walter Mignolo, in his study of literacy, territoriality, and colonization, writes: "The celebration of the letter and its complicity with the book were not only a warranty of truth but also offered the foundations for Western assumptions about the necessary relations between alphabetic writing and history. People without letters were thought of as people without history, and oral narratives were looked at as incoherent and inconsistent."[8]

In a different colonial context, Ranajit Guha, in his study of rural insurgency in colonial India, draws attention to "the peasant's hatred for the written word." Guha writes: "He had learnt, at his own cost, that the rent roll could deceive; that the bond could keep him and his family in almost perpetual servitude; that official papers could be used by clerks, judges, lawyers, and landlords to rob him of his land and livelihood. Writing was thus, to him, the sign of his enemy."[9] During slavery in the United States, it was illegal in various states for Black people to learn to read and write. "The most common known punishment for pursuing such learning was amputation."[10]

Colonial administrators, generals, slave traders, police, landowners, philosophers, novelists, and poets all used alphabetic writing as an essential tool of domination while simultaneously denying the depravity of their violence by denying the humanity of their victims.[11] This is one of the fundamental wounds of colonial history, but it was not opened nor maintained by the mere existence of letters, printing presses, or bookbinding. As José Rabasa writes in his study of historiography and conquest: "The colonizing force of alphabetical writing resides in the ideologies that inform its dissemination and the rules that implement scriptural projects, rather than in the technology itself."[12] Such ideologies and scriptural projects promoted physical invasion, enslavement, murder, torture, rape, racial hierarchies, and other forms of terror. In the grip of these ideologies that so loudly proclaimed values of liberty and democracy, writers and soldiers were not entirely distinguishable from one another.

As Ranajit Guha writes in his essay "The Prose of Counter-Insurgency": "The historian's attitude to rebels is in this instance indistinguishable from that of the State—the attitude of the hunter to his quarry."[13]

> Regarded thus an insurgent is not a subject of understanding or interpretation but of extermination, and the discourse of history, far from being neutral, serves directly to instigate official violence. [. . .] In this affinity with policy historiography reveals its character as a form of colonialist knowledge.[14]

Guha's reflections come in the context of a detailed analysis of a British historian's 1953 book on the 1799 Chuar Rebellion against British colonial power in India. His observations are also useful here and now for the person writing about the insurgents of the contemporary world. Reproducing the State's attitude to insurgents supports State violence against them—torture, forced disappearance, murder, massacre—as well as the epistemic violence necessary for ongoing colonial policies. When a writer or journalist identifies and rejects the hunter's, or the land speculator's, gaze and colonialist knowledge, what does he or she become?

"What gives journalism its authenticity and vitality," writes Janet Malcolm in her book *The Journalist and the Murderer*, "is the tension between the subject's blind self-absorption and the journalist's skepticism. Journalists who swallow the subject's account whole and publish it are not journalists but publicists."[15] The combination of "blind self-absorption" and "publicist" makes it seem as if Malcolm assumes that any individual speaking to a journalist is doing so willingly in a capitalist marketplace of ideas and stories. That is, that any such person is just trying to sell something. A journalist's skepticism is thus necessary for Malcolm to extract something interesting out of "blind self-absorption." Malcolm's assumption here exhibits, I think, one of the prime characteristics of the worldview and system of plunder known as "whiteness." Her assumption dissolves all possible differences of position into a universal standard of the "human" based on Malcolm and her white interviewees' particular experiences. (With one exception—Jeffrey Elliot, a white scholar of

Black studies—Malcolm only racially identifies Black people in her book—e.g., "a young black woman named Sheila Campbell," on page 44. Most of Malcolm's interviewees are white, though only one, Elliot, is explicitly identified as such. Providing racial identifiers for people of color while not providing them for white people is a standard practice of whiteness, one of many insidious and violent strategies of claiming "white" experience as universal.) In Malcolm's formulation, the "subject" and the "journalist" face each other in what would be theoretically a willing and equal relationship of power in the marketplace of ideas and stories. This assumption ignores, denies even, how race, gender, class, sexual orientation, language, age, and pain—so many "enmeshments of the body in time"[16]—structure the relationships of power between people in even the most seemingly mundane encounters, such as the relationships between people consenting to be interviewed for publication and people requesting to carry out such interviews.

I do not believe that everyone who participates in an interview with a journalist is essentially motivated by "blind self-absorption." Parents, for example, looking for their disappeared children or seeking justice for their murdered children will often consent to—and seek out—interviews as integral parts of their struggles, despite the pain brought up by the interviews. They want to find their disappeared children, or see their children's murderers punished, not promote themselves. I do not believe, for example, that a person who has survived torture and who is an active member of a clandestine guerrilla group, such as Andrés Tzompaxtle, could be said to heed "blind self-absorption" in consenting to be interviewed. For one, clandestine insurgents such as Tzompaxtle seek to conceal almost all details about their individual histories and lives to protect themselves from State repression. Tzompaxtle has granted three interviews in twenty-five years, and each time his desire to speak corresponded to making public his knowledge about State practices of torture and forced disappearance. He does not want to make his knowledge public to get tenure at a university; as he says quite clearly, he wants to help others who are fighting against those practices of State violence. To ask whether or not he also holds some degree of self-interest in presenting himself as a rebel seems to me offensive given the cause for the interview: What he has survived and the ongoing practices of State torture and forced disappearance. It seems to me that the "journalist's skepticism" in this context would be the equivalent of what Guha calls the attitude of the State, "the attitude of the hunter to his quarry." Avoiding such skepticism does not necessarily mean, however, being a publicist. Rather, I believe it means being an insurgent.

Some will say that a writer should not take sides, but should strive to remain objective. Such a response is insidious. Objectivity becomes, in practice, a mechanism for disguising official discourse, the discourse of power; in the hands of white writers, it becomes a mechanism for concealing and denying whiteness, for arrogantly and falsely claiming that a subjective text corresponds exclusively to objective facts and thus acquires the standing of some universal truth. From the moment a journalist or writer chooses to speak to one person and not another, to travel to one area and not another, to ask this question and not that question, to select this quote and not that quote, to use this adjective and not that one, the journalist is exercising subjectivity—decisions and values and desires—that structure and permeate the text. Objectivity is a ruse, and a dangerous and offensive one at that.

Honesty, in contrast, seems a value to which one can at least aspire. To be honest with the people about whom one plans to write and to be honest with one's readers about what one has written. And to be honest with oneself about one's own decisions, values, and desires and one's own particular standing in the power dynamics established through the very forms of violence one opposes, such as torture, racism, white supremacy, and patriarchy. Janet Malcolm, in her reflections on the journalist's craft, argues against absolute honesty with the person the journalist plans to write about. She writes that there is an essential act of deception at the heart of journalism:

> The catastrophe suffered by the subject is no simple matter of an unflattering likeness or a misrepresentation of his views; what pains him, what rankles and sometimes drives him to extremes of vengefulness, is the deception that has been practiced on him. On reading the article or book in question, he has to face the fact that the journalist—who seemed so friendly and sympathetic, so keen to understand him fully, so remarkably attuned to his vision of things—never had the slightest intention of collaborating with him on his story but always intended to write a story of his own. . . . [There is a] falseness built into the writer-subject relationship, about which nothing can be done. . . . Unlike other

relationships that have a purpose beyond themselves and are clearly delineated as such (dentist-patient, lawyer-client, teacher-student), the writer-subject relationship seems to depend for its life on a kind of fuzziness and murkiness, if not utter covertness, of purpose. If everybody puts his cards on the table, the game would be over. The journalist must do his work in a kind of deliberately induced state of moral anarchy.[17]

I do not want to settle into some "deliberately induced state of moral anarchy," assuming that Malcolm uses "anarchy" here to mean something like an unresolved contradiction. Nor am I convinced by the "tension between the subject's blind self-absorption and the journalist's skepticism." Perhaps she is correct, however, when she writes that if "everybody puts their cards on the table, the game would be over." Which leads me to ask: Might it not be better to stop that game and start something else?

Rather than the skepticism proposed by Malcolm, for me the vitality of journalism stems from leaving texts behind, for a time, and taking to the streets and the countryside to *listen* and to converse. Whoever assumes the attitude of the hunter does not listen so much as stalk to kill.

In his book *Writing Violence on the Northern Frontier*, José Rabasa asks: "To what extent can one write about violence without perpetuating it?"[18] In addressing this question, Rabasa develops the idea of "writing violence" to encompass both the act of writing about violence and the violence wielded by that writing. Rabasa explains this as follows:

The concept of writing violence comprises both the representations of massacres, tortures, rapes, and other forms of material terror, as well as categories and concepts informing the representation of territories for conquest, the definition of Indian cultures as inferior, and the constitution of colonized subjectivities. Whereas the first meaning of writing violence is self-evident, the second might provoke readers to resist seeing the force of writing itself as violence.[19]

Rabasa analyzes the writing of the Spaniards carrying out the violent invasion and conquest of territories that would be named "the Americas," including the writing of Spaniards critical of some aspects of Spanish colonial violence such as Bartolomé de las Casas in his 1552 book, *Brevíssima relación de la destruyción de las Indias*. Rabasa continues his investigation into the concept of writing violence as follows:

Descriptions of torture and terror lend themselves to a clarification of the materiality of writing violence. I can anticipate someone observing that there is an ontological difference between terrorizing someone and describing the torture in writing. But description can fulfill at least two functions: to instruct in techniques and to set an example. These modes of writing pertain to a culture of violence, but they also exercise material violence inasmuch as they have psychological impacts; the first forms the subjectivity of torturers (I assume a numbing of sensibilities), and the second aims to terrorize a population. . . . Description ensures a continuity of violence by shaping the sensibilities of those who will either endorse or commit future acts of terror.[20]

Rabasa analyzes the writings of different kinds of colonial administrators. What about, in 2017 as I work on the English-language edition of this book, the writing of anti-colonial insurgents? What about a writing that quite explicitly takes sides and seeks to "instruct in techniques and to set an example" not for police or torturers, but for insurgents, people and communities in struggle? As a writer quite conscientiously and openly taking a combative stance against colonial, capitalist, racist, and patriarchal violence, I ask myself Rabasa's question: "To what extent can one write about violence without perpetuating it?"[21] This question haunted me both as I spoke with and interviewed Tzompaxtle, as I sought a way of writing about his torture and forced disappearance, and as I translated and revised this book, always from my particular location in "the colonial matrix of power."[22]

Tzompaxtle told me several times that his knowledge, values, and strength did not come from books. He said this with pride and defiance. Considering that books were used as instruments of exclusion and violence against his ancestors, him, and his community, saying that he achieved what he did—surviving what he once described to me as "being pinned beneath a microscope of human cruelty"—without a "classical" education based in book learning, itself is a manner of rising up against cultural and epistemological exclusion, an affirmation of his culture, knowledge, and intelligence. Why would he need to affirm all that? Because we live in a world that continues to deny and attack it.

And yet Tzompaxtle was always reading. Every time I saw him he had a book with him. And we talked at length about those and other books: works of history, novels, and essays. It was clear that Tzompaxtle not only reads a lot, but that he reads with passion and devotion. That is, even though he did not form himself through book learning as a child and young man, he has added book learning to his ongoing self-formation. He confirmed what many have said and shown before: A guerrilla often has a book amongst the essential tools in his or her backpack.

Though alphabetic writing and the printed book have a horrid and murderous colonial history, they also have a beautiful, inspiring, and alive history of struggle. I am grateful beyond words for the books—the teachings, the sharing, the brilliance, the beauty, and the company—of so many fierce, unflinching, generous, and committed writers.

I aspire to join a long and ongoing movement to decolonize books, writing, and reading, to oppose all pretenses of cultural superiority and thinking that true, deep, or legitimate knowledge is transmitted through the written, printed, and bound word alone.

And with this book specifically—its reporting and research, its narrative structure, its writing and translation—I seek to build and offer a kind of embrace—an insurgent embrace—for words spoken and written in the literatures of struggle.

THE SOCIAL WORKER
AND THE LAWYER

In March 1997, the "Fray Francisco de Vitoria" Human Rights Center in Mexico City filed a written complaint with the Mexican National Human Rights Commission (CNDH), a federal governmental ombudsman of sorts, denouncing the forced disappearance of Andrés Tzompaxtle Tecpile. The Fray Vitoria Center was the only nongovernmental human rights organization to become directly involved in the case. I visited the organization's office in Mexico City and submitted a number of written requests to view the organization's archive on the case, but never received an answer. I was, however, able to interview a social worker, Balbina Flores, and a lawyer, Adriana Carmona, who worked for the Fray Vitoria in the 1990s. Together they wrote the complaint and worked on the case of Tzompaxtle's disappearance and the obligation of the State to investigate. At the time of this writing, Balbina Flores is the Mexico director of Reporters Without Borders. Adriana Carmona is a practicing lawyer and professor at the Autonomous University of Mexico City.

I interviewed Balbina Flores on July 18, 2013, in her

office. Flores showed little interest in my questions and repeatedly said, toward the end of our conversation, that this "was a strange case," clarifying when I questioned her that by "strange" she meant that Tzompaxtle's testimony seemed suspicious to her. Also, toward the end of the conversation, while she typed on her computer and I waited for her to continue telling me about a report that the Fray Vitoria Center put out in the 1990s about forced disappearances in Mexico, she said, out of nowhere, "And what is more, since his last name was so strange."

I was disturbed, to put it politely, to hear someone, much less a career human rights defender, utter such a racist trope. The last name Tzompaxtle Tecpile is a name native to the very patch of earth where we were sitting in that instant, that is, to Mexico City, a last name that existed in these lands long before the violent colonial arrival of Spanish last names like, for example, Flores. In 2007, Mexican writer Carlos Montemayor coordinated a dictionary of Náhuatl words used in Mexican Spanish.[1] The book, expanded and reprinted in 2009, was published by the National Autonomous University of Mexico and the Mexico Federal District Government. It contains 163 pages of single-word entries, eighty-eight pages of place-name entries, and thirty-nine pages of phrases. Náhuatl words such as tamales (plural), chocolate, nene, mole, molcajete, metate, mezcal, huapango, chingar, chipotle, chile, chicle, cacao, cacahuate, atole, apapachar, aguacate, peyote, popote, pulque, pozole, talacha, chamaco and chamaca, tequila, and tomate are essential to everyday spoken Spanish in Mexico, and many of these words, like chocolate, are now part of languages spoken all over the world. The greater Mexico City metropolitan area, not to mention the entire country, has thousands of names—municipalities, streets, neighborhoods, parks, and metro stations—in Náhuatl and scores of other indigenous languages. It is impossible to traverse the city—or the country—without speaking Náhuatl names and words. Here are only a few examples: Tlalpan, Chapultepec, Juanacatlán, Acapulco, Oaxaca, Azcapotzalco, Xochimilco, Tlatelolco, Cuauhtémoc, Nezahualcóyotl, Ecatepec, Teotihuacán, Chilpancingo, Coyoacán, Tenochtitlan, Mazatlán, Popcatépetl, and Tláhuac. And then, of course, there is the ubiquitous name of the country, the city, and the surrounding state: México, a Náhuatl word meaning, the place of the Mexica. So what precisely could be "strange" about the last name Tzompaxtle Tecpile? Unless the word "strange" serves to distance, denigrate, and deny; that is, to perpetrate colonial violence.

But before Flores said that, when I had just entered her office, I asked her if she would share with me what she remembered about the disappearance of Andrés Tzompaxtle Tecpile and her working on the case for the Fray Vitoria Center. She spoke for just over seven minutes. This is what she said:

> Well, at that time, around 1996, '97, I think it was, the Zapatista uprising had already happened. So with the atmosphere of the Zapatista uprising, the appearance of the EPR in Guerrero obviously, the political atmosphere was quite tense. Especially for the organizations working in human rights, like the Vitoria Center, and those of us who were there.

So, yes, there was a certain atmosphere of fear amongst social leaders and organizations, relative to the State's perception of certain people. Also around that time the Mesino family was arrested, if I'm not mistaken. There were other disappearances. Rafael's wasn't the only one. Later, years later, other EPR leaders were arrested.

So, obviously the EPR's emergence, which I think was in 1996, if I'm not mistaken, in Aguas Blancas, attracted attention, beyond Chiapas, also to Guerrero and to what was forming there, what was happening there. In this political context of everything that was going on, the case came to us, though I don't remember exactly how it came to us. I don't remember who brought it to us; I don't remember who called us or how it happened. The point is that a forced disappearance case showed up at the Vitoria Center. And, if I'm not mistaken, at the Vitoria Center we should have been working on a report. No. Not should have. We wrote a report, a short report about disappearances in Mexico. We took a couple of cases to talk about the issue, and one of the cases we took up was this one. How it happened, how they arrested him and after . . . I think in fact that the report was released by the Vitoria Center while he was still not free. I don't remember if he was disappeared for one or two years.

We never had direct contact with him after he appeared. I think we must have had contact with someone close to him, and that was how we learned about the events. With some relative or some close friend of his, that was how we knew about the case, about the disappearance and that he was a leader. And afterward, we submitted a complaint to the CNDH. The CNDH investigates, but obviously in doing so they sent the case file to SEDENA, the National Defense Secretariat. And I don't understand why, but SEDENA decides to subpoena us. The lawyer and I, who were the ones working closely on the case.

It was perhaps even a pretty dramatic affair, because in that era for civilians to go before a military tribunal as material witnesses in a case that you present as a human rights organization, well, it was quite unusual. We didn't know if it was really a part of the investigation or part of a pressure tactic to see whether or not we had direct links to him. At the end of the day what they wanted to know was where he was, if anyone knew that. Obviously, we did not know.

And so it was kind of traumatic in that sense, going to a tribunal and appearing as a witness in front of soldiers. I don't even remember where the appearance was. I don't know. I don't remember if it was at the Army base, or some Army office, I think near Polanco.

And, well, we went accompanied by our lawyer. What I remember is that the questions were in this line: if we knew him directly, how had we learned about the case, and how we got information about the disappearance.

We had sought legal counsel before going, and

we didn't go into any details. Nor did we really have much to tell. The truth is that it happened and was public. The Center decided to go public with our subpoena then because of all that it implied for human rights defenders to be called before a military tribunal about an investigation concerning human rights.

I don't remember if after that we kept . . . I don't know if we closed the case with the CNDH or if the investigation stayed open. What is certain is that he later appeared in a strange way. He appeared, I think, in the State of Mexico and made public the way in which he was able to escape from an Army base. I think it was an Army base near Teotihuacán, in the State of Mexico.

What I do remember is that he . . . gave a press conference and narrated how he was able to escape from the Army base. I don't recall his having established communication with us after he was able to escape. I understand that he went into hiding again on his own decision. And that was that.

Our appearance before the military tribunal was just an appearance, nothing more. We were witnesses and that's it. I don't have any more information.

I interviewed Adriana Carmona on two occasions at a café in Mexico City, first on June 19, 2013, and then on July 10, 2013. I asked her if she would share with me what she remembered about the forced disappearance of Andrés Tzompaxtle Tecpile and about her experiences working on the case. In the first interview, Carmona told me the following:

> I started working at the Fray Francisco de Vitoria Human Rights Center in 1993 and it was my first experience with human rights work. Before that I had worked on other issues. And back then there weren't so many human rights organizations; it wasn't such a well-known area. I came across the Vitoria Center by sheer accident, through some nuns who put me in touch with the organization to take a workshop there. I went to the workshop and that put me in touch with the compañeros at the Vitoria Center. And I recall that at first I started collaborating with them on several agrarian issues that they had at the time.
>
> Once I became a staff member at the Center, I learned its history of supporting Salvadoran immigrants fleeing harassment from the Salvadoran government for having participated in guerrilla movements, for having fought in the war in El Salvador. The Vitoria Center was founded by Benjamín Cuéllar, Monsignor Romero's lawyer. At first it was called Legal Aid (Socorro Jurídico).
>
> The Center's work consisted in supporting the immigrants, bringing them here, and helping with their applications for refugee status with the Office of the United Nations High Commissioner for Human Rights. Balbina Flores was the Center's social worker at that time, and she had a lot of experience working with those kinds of cases. When I started

working at the Center, we worked on a case involving a Salvadoran person who was somewhat related to guerrilla activity and was interned in the November 20 Hospital here in Mexico City. That was my first contact, my first experience with . . . We went to speak with the person in the hospital to document the case, and as we left federal government agents started following us.

And, well, I didn't know anything about that kind of thing, but you quickly get used to being followed, having your phone tapped, and hearing those strange sounds on the phone line. So, we had some experience with that kind of harassment for working on human rights cases. And at that time, human rights work wasn't as well known as it is now. In fact, they called us, "people from human resources."

So I started working with the Center in 1993. And then [the Zapatista uprising in] 1994 was a new experience for all of us in human rights. We started working on case documentation. And also in 1994, international organizations start working in Mexico, which hadn't really happened before. International organizations hadn't been very interested in the human rights situation in Mexico before that. Before then, Mexico had a good image internationally as a country that respects human rights. In 1994 that image was fractured, despite the then-recent creation of the National Human Rights Commission (CNDH). The truth is that the international human rights organizations turned to look at Mexico after the Zapatista uprising.

And so we started documenting cases of arbitrary executions, working closely with the Fray Bartolomé de las Casas Human Rights Center. A number of organizations also founded a network of human rights organizations called the Human Rights Network All Rights For All. At the time almost all the human rights organizations in the country had some relation with the church. That's why we organized brigades to Chiapas and the human-shield peace missions [cinturones de la paz], and case documentation all in collaboration with other organizations. Around that time the first cases against Mexico for human rights violations were taken before the Inter-American Commission on Human Rights, with the legal aid of the Minnesota Advocates for Human Rights. Physicians for Human Rights started coming to Mexico. This contact with international organizations helped us with tools and experience in human rights defense.

And it was in this context that we got the case. Though, wait, before that: After 1994 there started being problems in Guerrero and Oaxaca. These issues weren't as well documented. At the Vitoria Center we published annual reports on the human rights situation in Mexico. Through this analysis we saw that there was a human rights crisis in Mexico with torture, abuse, arbitrary detentions, and those kinds of cases. These were the kinds of cases we were taking on: torture, abuse, and arbitrary detention.

And so it was in this context, and working on

those types of cases, that we received a sealed en-
velop with Andrés's case, to give it a name. A sealed
envelope arrived at the most visible human rights
organizations of the time, the strongest, which
were the Comisión Mexicana with Mariclaire Acosta, the Miguel Agustín Pro Juárez Human Rights
Center with David Fernández, and us at the Vitoria
Center. As I recall, the envelope—it was large, le-
gal-document size, yellow—arrived at those three
organizations. Someone left the envelope for us at
the Cultural Center.* When someone brought the
envelope up to us, we had no idea what it was about.
But, well, when Marisol López, Balbina Flores, and
I opened it, we were in charge of the legal department, we had a lot of discussions, including other
people at the Center, about what we should do with
that envelope.

We were facing a serious challenge considering
that the issue was directly and openly related to the
guerrillas and involved investigating the Army. But
what we were concerned about was how to respond
to an action that we considered a serious violation
of human rights. That is, it didn't matter if he was or
wasn't a guerrilla. The issue was arbitrary detention
and, most of all, disappearance, where the man's life
was at risk. We had a very intense discussion about
all this. We argued a lot about this with Mariclaire

---

* The Fray Vitoria Human Rights Center's offices are located inside
the University Cultural Center on the campus of the National Autonomous University of Mexico.

and David, I recall. Because this wasn't like the typical case with Zapatismo where people detained and tortured formed parts of solidarity committees and didn't have anything to do with the armed movement. This case did involve an armed movement. And that sparked a serious discussion about whether we should take the case on or not.

I remember now that Amnesty International had the policy, which they still do, that political prisoners couldn't have anything to do with armed movements. So Amnesty International didn't take cases like this, by its own statutes. Amnesty International will never recognize a political prisoner, or a case of human rights violations when the person is involved with armed movements.

At first we tried to promote all three human rights organizations carrying out initial inquiries. We put out a press release signed by the three organizations. But when it came time to submit the complaint before the National Human Rights Commission, the other two organizations didn't want to participate. So we once again discussed the issue inside the Vitoria, and decided that we could submit the complaint appealing to the National Human Rights Commission's obligation to investigate and to protect the personal information of those who submit the complaint. That gave us some protection, so to speak, to go before them and request that they investigate the issue.

So we started to document the case and we sent what we had along with what had been sent to us, all the information we had while Andrés was still disappeared. When he was able to escape and sent the video with his testimony, we added all that information to the complaint before the National Commission. But during the whole time of documentation after we submitted the complaint, we kept getting calls and letters from the National Commission requesting that we take the person named in the complaint to them, that we introduce them to the people who had given us the information. We repeatedly informed them that we did not have any contact beside the written information we had received. Obviously, we were afraid that they would try to link us to the armed movement. And we had to make it very clear that our role was exclusively as human rights defenders, and that we didn't have anything to do with armed movements. But . . . the National Human Rights Commission always takes a long time to investigate, but they were also hesitant to make a recommendation against SEDENA. Even after Andrés escaped and gave his testimony about where he was detained and held and how he was tortured, the CNDH's hesitancy to really investigate was quite remarkable.

So it took forever for the CNDH to collect the information they had to request from SEDENA. In all the other cases that we had before the CNDH we maintained direct communication with the lead investigator so that we could be kept abreast of the information coming in and contribute further with our own research. We couldn't do that in this case.

Because rather than the CNDH giving us information, they were the ones harassing us.

At the same time that we were working on Andrés's case, we were doing research for a report on the CNDH's relationship with the Army. The CNDH had never made a recommendation against the Army for human rights violations. In our report we documented with concrete statistics how many complaints the CNDH had received against the Army and which violations soldiers were accused of committing. With those statistics we then showed that the National Human Rights Commission had not made one single recommendation against SEDENA. That was the main point of that report.

Another important thing for the context of that moment was that the Mexican government had just begun to receive the first recommendations of international human rights organizations for human rights violations related to the Zapatista uprising: torture and arbitrary detention. Ernesto Zedillo [Mexican president, 1994–2000] formed an interdepartmental commission, which opened the way for the first direct dialogue [between the Zapatistas and] the authorities, the PGR [Attorney General], and I think SEDENA was at one meeting. We asked for them to follow up on the human rights recommendations made against them. All that, I think, helped push the CNDH to make a recommendation against the Army.

After the recommendation, Balbina and I received subpoenas to appear before the Military

Justice Attorney General [Procuraduría de Justicia Militar]. Such an appearance, obviously, worried us a whole, whole lot. We put out a press release to let the media know what was happening. We requested that the CNDH send a representative to accompany us. We also received support from Mexico City's Human Rights Commission, because we were obviously worried about our safety and about how the gathering of our testimony would be carried out. That was the first time that someone from a human rights organization was subpoenaed to testify before the Military Justice Attorney General. Before that, a number of lawyers took cases before the Military Justice Attorney General, but in Chiapas, not here at their headquarters.

So yes, we were really afraid that we would suffer some attack. We went, and the procedure took a long time, like three hours. And during the procedure, the military prosecutor takes out the complete case file, including the videos we had given to the CNDH. According to the CNDH's rules and regulations, it is absolutely prohibited to turn over information. They have to safeguard all the complainant's information, for example, information about us and the Center. And then we realized that the Military Justice Attorney General had all that information, that they had the entire case file. And the prosecutor's questions—more than twenty questions—tried to link us to the armed movement. The whole time it was: "And when you spoke with the person named in the complaint . . . and when you corresponded with the person named in the complaint." And after every question we had to clarify: "I must say that we have not had contact with the person named in the complaint beyond the written correspondence and that we do not have any relation to any kind of armed movement." A large part of the testimony went like that. It was really tense and, obviously, very intimidating and irritating.

After that experience we sent a letter of complaint to the CNDH for their having given the entire case file, including our entire original complaint, to SEDENA, as well as for having been subpoenaed. That document didn't have even the smallest impact. If I remember correctly, they never even responded to us. So no, nothing came of that letter.

Afterward we never knew if the Army made some kind of statement or punished someone. Truthfully, I don't remember hearing anything about it at all. And I can't remember right now if the CNDH, that publishes follow-up reports on recommendations they've made, if they considered that their recommendation was heeded or not. I don't recall how that recommendation was classified.

After that case and our involvement in it, we were faced with the situation in Oaxaca and the appearance of the guerrillas in Crucecita. After that there were a lot of cases of disappearance and extrajudicial executions in Oaxaca. The Vitoria

Center together with the Mexican Human Rights League and Action Against Torture (I don't know if that last organization, ACAT, still exists) started to document cases in Oaxaca. The cases of forced disappearance that we documented in Oaxaca, I remember, had a similar modus operandi, to put it that way, as Andrés's case. That is, Army agents arrived, forced the person into a car, blindfolded them, and took them to a location to be interrogated by other agents. After being interrogated they were taken to another location, obviously having been beaten and tortured.

I remember that during that time there were disappearances daily and we submitted appeals almost by the pound, an impressive amount of appeals sent by fax. But almost all the people later reappeared. I remember that only two people didn't appear, and one of them appeared a year later. I don't remember where. But that person who appeared a year later gave testimony that they kept him in one place and tortured him, but then later they moved him to an Army base where they made him wash soldiers' clothes. He was the one washing the sheets and clothes and who knows what. But he left; he was able to get out of that place. And that is the only case I recall of someone appearing after such a long disappearance.

Carmona told me about some other jobs she did after leaving the Vitorio Center where she had to argue cases before the Military Justice Attorney General, experiences that reaffirmed that "the experience we had was totally anomalous, and was not in accordance with the way military justice should function, but was actually just a long interrogation."

I then asked her if she remembered what was in that first envelope that arrived at the Center.

First, the envelope contained letters with all the information. We also received in that first complete document the information about the car that he left behind, the Volkswagen, the same one that later appeared. We received very concrete information that could be used for a detailed investigation. They also sent us a video with his wife's testimony. She described how he was disappeared. And when he appeared we received the other video. I don't think we got a letter with that video. I can't remember if we got a letter as well. But we did get the video where he describes his abduction, torture, and the mistreatment he suffered. And, as well, giving really detailed indications about where he was held. I think SEDENA was looking into that information. And I think he was trying to implicate the officers at the military base in Teotihuacán.

And, in fact, it wasn't so well known back then that there was a military base there. Now it is. But at that time SEDENA didn't acknowledge that there was a base there. I don't recall, because we didn't go there until later, so I don't recall how developed it was. That was a subject of debate. Today we know. Every time I go by there I think about this case, because now the base is more built up.

I asked her if she had gone to inspect the area at the time.

After [hearing Tzompaxtle's testimony], yes. The only way to see it was by climbing up the Pyramid of the Sun. It wasn't easy to get access. Because the base is right there in the middle of San Juan de Teotihuacán. I mean, now the base is well established and built up there. Back then it wasn't so developed. So you had to climb up the Pyramid of the Sun, and from that height you could see a bit of the base being built. I don't think it was so built up like it is now.

The details that he gave were absolutely true. The distances that he described about how far he walked, how he arrived, where he asked for help. All of that description held up in fact. What is more, you know, with a good investigation, which military justice should have had to carry out, you could have easily found those responsible.

And . . . I think it was one of the first testimonies, which would later be repeated in Oaxaca, that described how such torture and forced disappearances were part of military intelligence operations used to investigate armed movements. It was a systematic operation that was in violation of human rights, as we all know, and it wasn't that new either.

The first disappeared in Mexico were related to the cases that Rosario Ibarra de Piedra documented, and they all shared the same mechanics, that is, the same ways of acting.

With the Vicente Fox administration [2000–2006] some of these things start to get modified, but the modus operandi, let's say, continued. That is, that's how the government operates.

I asked her what she thought to be the relation between those cases of forced disappearance and what was happening at the time of our interview in 2013.

With the disappearances during the Calderón administration [2006–2012] the argument is, "they're involved in drug trafficking" and that makes everything permissible. . . . And the people they are disappearing . . . I think before they were much more selective with disappearances, and now the idea is to cause terror in the population so that no one moves, no one even thinks about talking. So they disappear anyone.

During this last stage of the Calderón administration, at least in Chihuahua, I think there is a lot of frustration, because there really no longer exists even the minimum rule of law capable of dealing with all this. For example, if you say that you'll take a case against the government to the Inter-American Commission, the government couldn't care less. In the 1990s that had an impact. Today it doesn't. And I think that today the human rights organizations have to rethink their strategies, because this government, both the outgoing Calderón administration and the return of the PRI in the next administration, they're coming at us with everything they've got. And they don't care anymore about their image with the international organizations.

AN INCREDIBLE ESCAPE

HERE'S ONE. THE YEAR IS 1978. Argentina. The military dictatorship is in full swing. The military and police death squads operate with absolute freedom. They have built semi-hidden concentration camps across the country where they disappear, torture, and murder. Four young men have been disappeared for months inside a clandestine torture center known as the Seré Mansion in the city of Morón, province of Buenos Aires. The men are handcuffed and bound with leather straps. They are completely naked, bearing all the marks, bruises, and burns left by a team of torturers not at all worried about leaving scars. Their captors recently cut their hair short but left their beards of four months. The men have bathed two or three times in 120 days, but have not been allowed to brush their teeth. They have lived on two meals a day and no exercise. It is March 24, after midnight. The four men are in a room on the second story of the mansion. The two overnight guards are downstairs. One of the men has been practicing removing his thinned wrists from his handcuffs. He also found a loose screw while being forced to clean the house one day and hid it under his mattress. He pulls his hands out of the handcuffs, unties himself

195

and removes the screw. One by one his companions untie themselves, though they all still remain handcuffed. The first man takes the three blankets in the room, rolls them up lengthwise and ties them together with the leather straps, making a kind of rope. He then takes the screw, slides it through the window latch where the torturers had removed the handle, and uses it to open the window. He unties and opens the external blinds and climbs out onto the balcony, ties the impromptu rope to a column, and drops it toward the ground. Three of the men climb—naked, bruised, unbathed, malnourished, and handcuffed—down the blanket and leather strap line and then drop about two meters to the ground. The man who made the rope and opened the window is the last to descend. Before doing so, he takes his screw and scratches into the wall of the room: "Thanks, Lucas!" a farewell message to one of the torture center's cruelest guards. Then he too climbs down. Now the four naked men leave the property without anyone seeing or hearing them. They run through the predawn streets, try and fail to hotwire two cars, before hiding in a small construction site in the residential neighborhood. The young man who found the screw had unrolled the T-shirt used to blindfold him and put it on. He leaves the hiding place, walks a few steps and knocks on a door, asking a woman who peeks through the window for help, saying that he has just been robbed. He asks her to call his uncle's house. She does, but no one answers. He repeats his misfortune of having no money to get home and being stripped mostly naked. She gives him a pair of pants and some money for a cab. He goes back to the hiding place to tell the others he will send a car for them.

He then goes back outside, walks a few blocks, stops a taxi and leaves. Helicopters begin to fly overhead, combing the area. Within minutes, however, it starts raining and then the rain becomes a major thunderstorm and forces the helicopters to suspend their flight. The young man who found the screw is able to call the father of one of the other three men and give him directions to the hiding spot, where he finds them the following morning. They all escape and spend months in hiding. One at a time, and independently, three of the four leave the country. The other is captured again, disappeared, but then liberated after the fall of the dictatorship in 1983.

One of the survivors who escaped that day is Claudio Tamburrini, a former professional soccer player and now philosophy professor in Stockholm. A few years ago he wrote a book about his abduction, torture, and escape called *Pase libre: La fuga de la Mansión Seré* (Free Pass: The Escape from the Seré Mansion). The young man who found the screw is an actor now living in Paris. In 2006, he played the head torturer in a film based on Tamburrini's book called *Crónica de una fuga* (Chronicle of an Escape).[1] In this film, Guillermo Fernández plays the part of "The Judge," a high-level government torturer who tells the young Guillermo Fernández in the film that he has a week to tell everything he knows, everything he'd kept hidden up to then, or be killed, painfully.

Theirs was the only confirmed escape from a clandestine torture center during the Argentine military dictatorship of 1976–1983. Three of the four survivors testified during the trials against the military junta in 1985.

Here's another one, this time from the waning years of the dictatorship of Augusto Pinochet in Chile. Two political prisoners, both members of the Frente Patriótico Manuel Rodríguez guerrilla movement, start by scratching their cell wall with a fork. Within a few hours they have a handful of dust. Two months later they have a 50-centimeter hole. Then they are transferred to a different cell. They hide their work before leaving, recruit a few new comrades and start over. It is now July 1988. By January 29, 1990, a total of twenty-four political prisoners have been working around the clock in shifts to dig an eighty-meter tunnel from their prison cell, circumnavigating the subway tube, and into the street near an abandoned train station. The tunnel was equipped with ventilation, electricity, radio communication, and an improvised railcar for removing dirt from the tunnel (which the prisoners then passed through a hole in their cell's ceiling to comrades in the cell above them who hid the dirt by spreading it out in a crawl space between their cell's ceiling and the prison roof).[2] The prisoners had coordinated with their comrades on the outside to set off a series of small bombs far from the prison on the night of their escape, pick up the escapees at the train station in an old bus, and deliver them to safe houses spread out across Santiago. Within an hour and a half of crawling out of the dirt they are all safely distributed and hidden. Before that, though, once they had all emerged from the tunnel, one of them crawled back into the prison—a fifteen-minute trip on elbows and knees along a 50-square-centimeter tunnel—approached a group of political prisoners who had not participated in nor known about the escape plan, and told them: "Listen: Get ready for tomorrow, because there will be a CNI search. Some of us won't be here. We left the door open."[3] He then hurried back to the hole and escaped. It then takes the other prisoners about two hours to find the hole and decide to risk what may be a trap: Nineteen of them make it—amazed, bewildered, terrified, covered in dirt, and then elated—another six are recaptured. What began with a few hours of scratching a prison wall with a fork led, through incredible discipline and ingenuity, to forty-three political prisoners escaping from prison in the middle of the nation's capital during the final official days of the Pinochet dictatorship.

Or how about this one? The year is 1971, in Uruguay. One hundred and eleven prisoners, all members of the Tupamaro urban guerrilla movement, dig a 44-meter tunnel from the Punto Carretas prison into the living room of a house across the street. They and five other prisoners all escape.

And, well, David Kaplan left the Santa Martha Acatitla prison in Mexico City when a helicopter descended into the prison courtyard, retrieving Kaplan and a friend and then flying them to the northern border on August 19, 1971.[4]

On January 19, 2001, Joaquín Loera Guzmán was either smuggled out in a laundry cart or simply walked through the door of the Puente Grande maximum-security prison in Jalisco. Either way, he left without leaving a trace.[5] And then, of course, he would be recaptured in February 2014 and once again exit a maximum-security prison, the impenetrable Almoloya in Mexico State, on July 11, 2015. This time he either climbed down a sixty-foot-deep hole from the floor of his cell-room shower—just out of a twenty-four-hour surveillance camera's angle of vision—and then rode his makeshift underground motorcycle railcar down a mile-long tunnel and climbed back up into a shoddy, unfinished cinderblock house built a year before, apparently for the express and sole purpose of receiving just this visit, or, again, maybe he just walked out the door.[6]

And, well: On May 16, 2009, some twenty armed men with Federal Preventive Police and Federal Investigative Agency uniforms and vehicles released fifty-three prisoners—all caught smiling by the surveillance cameras—from the Cieneguillas prison in Zacatecas, Mexico.[7] On March 26, 2010, forty-one prisoners escaped in Matamoros. Twelve escaped in Reynosa on April 2, 2010, and another twelve escaped on July 7.[8] In September 2010, another eighty-five prisoners escaped in Reynosa, and in December 2010, 141 prisoners escaped in Nuevo Laredo.[9] Journalist Luis Carlos Sáinz counted 451 prison breaks with 1,512 escaped prisoners between 2000 and 2011.[10] In September 2012, 132 prisoners escaped from the Piedras Negras prison in Coahuila. They dug a tunnel from the prison's carpentry workshop and walked out into the street at 2:15 p.m.[11] Or maybe not? Some say that the 132 prisoners walked out the front door.[12] Did they?

Omar Guerrero Solís, better known as Comandante Ramiro of the Insurgent People's Revolutionary Army (ERPI), escaped twice. Once when federal police were taking him to the state prison in Acapulco: As they were driving over a bridge, Ramiro—handcuffed—managed to open the car door, dive out, and jump off the bridge into the Balsas River, swollen with recent heavy rains. He swam away. The government caught him again years later and put him in jail in Coyuca de Catalán, brutally torturing him for days on end, urinating on his beaten face. But in time he organized the prisoners there, slowly wresting control of the place from the warden and the guards. So they moved him to a large, rough prison in Acapulco—beating him throughout the car ride—and arranged to have him killed by other prisoners. That day he looked his killers in the eyes and said: "The first one to make a move is coming with me." His killers paused. And then they listened. Commander Ramiro organized the prisoners there and held a series of protests. Local reporters went to the prison to cover the story. The warden called him to his office and asked what would shut him up. Ramiro said he had planned to denounce the prison guards' drug dealing racket, but would be content if the warden granted three demands: one, no guards would enter his cell; two, give the prisoners tools to create a woodshop and allow them to sell their wares to visiting family members; and three, remove the guard from the tower overlooking his cell. That, he said, would keep him quiet. The warden said, "done," and granted all three demands. Ramiro called off the protests and, together with some of the prisoners first hired to kill him, over the course of several months dug a twenty-meter-long tunnel under the Guerrero State Prison in Acapulco through which he crawled out into the sunshine on November 28, 2002.[13]

THE BROTHERS

THIS IS WHAT THE POLICE said: the Federal Preventive Police (PFP) officers José Antonio Palacios Beristáin and Roberto Armenta Romero were traveling along México-Veracruz Highway 150-D between Orizaba and Fortín when they saw a car parked on the shoulder of the highway "partially invading the right traffic lane, without any kind of warning flags."[1] It was 10:30 in the morning.

The police saw five men inside the vehicle, a 2001 Volkswagen sedan with Veracruz plates. The police stopped and approached the driver, who identified himself with his Federal Electoral Institute (IFE) identification card under the name Gerardo Tzompaxtle Tecpile. The driver also handed over his vehicle registration card and told the police:

> [The car was] broken down with a mechanical failure (overheated motor), for which reasons the officers [offered to] help pushing the automobile off of the pavement surface using their patrol car for the safety of the people in the car and those traveling on the highway, after which they asked the driver where the men were heading and who were the other people

in the car, the driver stated that he did not know the passengers and that he was only giving them a ride, in this moment two passengers got out of the car and said they were going to buy water in town and walking quickly they went into the population center of Buenavista, Veracruz, that is located there near the highway, continuing the interview, the passengers who remained were MR. GUSTAVO ROBLES LÓPEZ, 29-year-old Mexican [. . .] and a man who identified himself as JORGE MARCIAL TZOMPAXTLE TECPILE—being the brother of the driver—a 36-year-old Mexican, and who has the same address as the driver in Astacinga, Veracruz, and who did not offer any identification.[*]

The police ordered the remaining three men to get out of the car and interrogated them separately. The police claim that the men contradicted each other, with one man saying that they were going to "the 'SORIANA' shopping center, this being false as in said city there is no such shopping center of that company." Another of the men said, the police claim, that they were on their way to Córdoba "to screw some broads [sic] and then go back to Orizaba." As a result of these contradictions, the police searched the car:

---

[*]   Quotations from the police document Parte Informativo de Servicios No. 043/2006 appear here mostly as they do in the original, including some grammar errors. I corrected a number of the police report's spelling and punctuation errors in the process of translation, as it seemed too forced to try to reproduce those Spanish language errors in the English translation. A few words are illegible in the scanned copy I have on file and are represented with ellipses here.

finding five cellular telephones, a photography camera and a video camera, in the vehicle's trunk five backpacks containing various articles of clothing and shoes were found, bandannas were found in one of the backpacks—one of them camouflage. For this reason backup was sought from the shift and patrol manager to conduct a more exhaustive search of the vehicle and its occupants.

Five PFP patrol cars with eight officers of various ranks arrived. The police report continues:

Upon conducting a more thorough search, agents found inside one of the backpacks—of blue color and the brand NICKS CLUB [sic]—a notebook-style datebook inside of which different meetings and activities in Guerrero and Veracruz states were handwritten, on one page dated November 2005, located in Guerrero state, the handwriting says:

"[. . .] we have followed the developments of the past months closely. Events in which you all participated. For which reason, considering the possibility of you all receiving my modest [. . .]

"First to tell you all that I do not have knowledge as to the arguments and strategy you all used to carry out some of the activity [sic] and thus I can resort to mere speculation clearing this up concerning the above; I move on the next issue.

"You all carry out the oak tree action, and that much is fine. And it is here where I ask myself some questions. Why did you not claim responsibility for said action as such and you pull some unknown logo out of your sleeve? And then the communiqué as LPEP. Was it necessary to say that there was a list of "candidates" condemned to the maximum punishment? And on the other hand in that moment of vendettas between the drug cartels the action is perceived (at first) as a result of the fighting between mafias.

"Later on a series of bickering between you all and the hawkish ones, owing on the one hand to the elimination of 'x' whom we all know was a problem for everyone in the movement."

The police report continues as follows:

Asking the driver MR. GERARDO TZOMPAX-TLE TECPILE what the written notes meant he answered that he would give us all the money he had with him if we let them go on their way—because he couldn't talk about the content of the date-book—that he had about $4,500.00 (four thousand five hundred and 00/100 pesos in national currency). MR. GUSTAVO ROBLES LÓPEZ offered the amount of $2,500.00 (two thousand and 00/100 pesos in national currency) as well because we let them go and MR. JORGE TZOMPAXTLE TECPILE, who also offered the amount of $2,000.00 (two thousand and 00/100 pesos in national currency) for which reason, for this we took them to the police station offices in Orizaba, we communicated via telephone with Mr. Ramiro Espinosa Jiménez, regional sub delegate of the National Center for Investigation and Security (CISEN) in Guerrero state to ask for his help in the investigation of the above mentioned people.

The police also called the CISEN director in Veracruz to inform him of "the situation of the people and the documents found in the automobile so he would be able to carry out the corresponding investigation."

On the next page, the police report mentions an annexed document "that in the fourth paragraph establishes the relationship between these brothers in direct line of action to the so-named combatant Rafael from the Popular Revolutionary Army, (EPR)."

The media mostly followed the police description of the events that day on the highway in Veracruz. On January 13, 2006, Iván González from *Noticieros Televisa* published an article with the headline: "PFP arrests three alleged members of the EPR." The article begins like this:

> The Federal Attorney General's (PGR) office is investigating three alleged members of the Popular Revolutionary Army (EPR) arrested this Wednesday by Federal Preventive Police officers in Veracruz.
>
> The men in question are Gustavo Robles López, alias Commander Robles, and the brothers Gerardo and Jorge Marcial Tzompaxtle Tecpile.

The men were arrested due to their suspicious attitude on kilometer 28 of the México-Veracruz highway, between Orizaba and Fortín.

According to the police report to the federal prosecutors, the PFP found the men in possession of subversive material, such as communiqués from Commander Rafael of the EPR, photographs and a datebook with telephone numbers written in it, five backpacks with bandannas and military-style uniforms, as well as cellular telephones.

The PGR is investigating the possible participation of the men arrested in the June 2003 kidnapping of Veracruz Congressman Mario Zepahua.

The article concludes by stating that the three men were being held in Orizaba waiting for a possible transfer to Mexico City.

That same day, January 13, Juan H. Santos published an article on the website *Orizaba en Red* with the headline: "CISEN confirms that Gerardo Tzompaxtle is actually Commander Rafael" and two subheadings: "Yes, the men arrested in Orizaba are connected to the EPR" and "SIE-DO [former acronym for the federal anti–organized crime investigative task force] agents will transfer the arrested to Mexico City." The article begins with this line:

Speaking unofficially, an agent from the National Center for Investigation and Security (CISEN) confirmed, this Friday afternoon, that Gerardo Tzompaxtle Tecpile, from the nearby community of Astacinga, in the Zongolica mountains of Veracruz state, is known in the subversive movement of the Popular Revolutionary Army (EPR) as Commander Rafael.

The reporter includes information about Gerardo Tzompaxtle's date of birth and school records provided by the PGR. He then writes:

> CISEN corroborated unofficially [sic] that Gerardo Tzompaxtle Tecpile, Commander Rafael, escaped from a military base in Mexico City; moreover, his cousins Jorge and Gaspar are members of the PRD in the Zongolica region.

Also on that same day, January 13, a letter signed by the "Tzompaxtle Tecpile Family" arrived at various media outlets. The letter stated the following:

> The family of brothers Jorge Marcial and Gerardo respectfully address you all in order to clarify the facts about the arrests.
>
> Yesterday, Thursday, January 12 of the current year, Jorge and Gerardo were traveling from Astacinga to Córdoba to shop at the Aurrerá supermarket. It is well known that our family owns and operates a store. However their car broke down near the pedestrian bridge Buena Vista over the Orizaba-Córdoba highway. They were traveling in Gerardo's gray 2001 Jetta with Veracruz license plate number YCD-19-41. A Federal Preventive Police patrol car, far from offering help, addressed them

arrogantly, humiliating them. They tried to defend their human rights, leading the police to begin to threaten and blackmail them and to begin "planting evidence" such as the farce published today in the media, all of this a true act of calumny.

Our family members are being arrested, we insist, arbitrarily since the supposed "proof" could be found in the files of any police department and the rest is information that appears in print and online media. Thus we categorically deny all the charges made against them. We also state that it is customary for the police to charge any innocent citizen with a thousand crimes that as time passes all get dropped and their innocence proven with barely an apology. And who will repair all the damage done? We also demand that their properties be respected and their vehicle returned.

It is impossible that in less than twelve hours the police could develop a supposed "investigation" built on twenty years' work, when none of the arrested have any criminal record. The police present landscape photographs like that of the Citlaltépetl volcano or photographs of historic monuments like the iron palace in Orizaba which, according to the police farce, could be used to plan "attacks." Only a perverse mind could make up such a cock-and-bull story. Over the following days we will disprove with facts all of these calumnies.

We repeat: our family members are being taken as scapegoats. The police arrest and jail anyone who takes their picture, but does nothing against the real criminals.

Thus we respectfully and humbly ask the human rights defense organizations to assist our family members, not to let them go undefended, as they are surely being physically and psychologically tortured. We also ask lawyers aware of these dynamics to offer the necessary pro bono legal assistance.

On April 25, 2006, the PGR issued bulletin 535/06: "Preventive detention for three alleged members of EPR." The bulletin begins:

The Third District Federal Court Judge in the Federal District issued an order for the preventive detention of Gerardo Tzompaxtle Tecpile, Jorge Marcial Tzompaxtle Tecpile, and Gustavo Robles López, alleged members of the Popular Revolutionary Army (EPR) operating in the mountains of Guerrero and Veracruz, for violation of the Federal Law Against Organized Crime.

The bulletin states that the evidence was gathered by the SIEDO for the PGR. It then states:

The accused are said to be members of a criminal organization linked to subversive groups, to whom they lent their apartments to recruit new members, they also took care that trainings were going well and they spread the cause.

Last January 13, Federal Preventive Police officers arrested Gerardo Tzompaxtle Tecpile, Jorge Marcial Tzompaxtle Tecpile, and Gustavo Robles López on the México-Córdoba highway, near the El Fortín tollbooth, in possession of propaganda documents alluding to the EPR, for which reason the officers turned them over to the SIEDO.

On September 30, Diego Osorno published an article in *Milenio Semanal* with the headline: "Revenge for Rafael's Escape." In the article, Osorno writes the following:

One of the Federal Highway Patrol officers who participated in the arrest confirmed that the capture of the alleged EPR guerrillas took place by accident. "The vehicle looked suspicious, so we approached it. A bit later we noticed that the people in the car were acting strangely, really nervous. We asked for their IDs and ran the names when we got a notice over the radio that the names corresponded to guerrillas."

This is what Gerardo Tzompaxtle Tecpile told me in an interview:

It was January 12, 2006. We left my hometown, Astacinga. We left at around six in the morning in my car. We went by the ADO bus station to pick up a friend of my brother Jorge, someone he's known for a long time. Then we went to drink some juice here in Orizaba, near the technological institute.

And there, as we were getting back in the car, two young guys asked me if I could give them a ride. And I said, "Sure, as far as Córdoba." I thought they were students at the institute. I studied there. Then we went to the highway entrance near the University Chemistry Department in Orizaba.

I asked him if he could describe the two young men. "They seemed like college students, somewhere between twenty and twenty-five years old," he told me, and then continued: "So then we got on the highway. And, what was it, maybe five kilometers? The car overheated and we pulled over. We got out to push the car to a safe place. A few moments later the feds arrived. They pulled up and stopped beside us and asked what had happened. 'Well, the car was overheating so we're pulling over.' So they followed us, as if they were escorting us."

Gerardo Tzompaxtle told me that the police officers were Federal Highway Patrol officers and that they never pushed his car with their patrol car. Rather, they pushed the car by hand. The police officers parked, got out of their patrol car and approached them. They looked over the five men, and then one of the officers said: "Okay, open the trunk." Gerardo Tzompaxtle got out of the driver's seat and opened the trunk with the key. At this moment the two young men said they were going to go for help. "Those guys wanted to help me out, they were being nice. There were some houses nearby. 'We'll go and see if they can give us some water or maybe help find a mechanic,' they said."

The two young men went walking along the shoulder of the highway. At the same time the police were looking through the things in the trunk. "They left without their backpacks," Gerardo Tzompaxtle told me. "We had put them in the trunk. The police started searching through the backpacks. I think it was in one of their backpacks that they found a datebook with some notes in it. That's when I realized that the police were calling on their radios, using police codes. About twenty or thirty minutes later more police started to arrive.

Before the other police officers arrived, the two highway patrol agents separated the three men who had stayed with the car—Gerardo, Jorge Tzompaxtle, and Gustavo Robles—and they started interrogating them. They asked Gerardo to identify himself and tell them where he was heading. "So I told them that we were going to Córdoba. They were really stubborn about asking why we were going to Córdoba and what were we going to do there. 'We're going to drink some beers, see some women friends, you know, hang out for a while.' Then the cop asked us: 'Whose datebook is this?'" Gerardo told him that the backpack where they found the datebook belonged to one of the two young guys.

"So you do know them," the police officer said.

"I mean, I saw them at the school, the technological institute, and I thought they were students."

"You know," the officer said, "tell the truth, because you do know them."

"If I knew them I'd take you to where they live, their house. But I don't know who they are."

"And this datebook is yours?"

"No."

"Yes it is. Admit it."

"How can I admit it?"

"You guys are fucked."

"Why," Gerardo asked him. "How much do I owe for the . . . give me a ticket. I mean, if I was a bit . . . I wasn't intentionally blocking the road. The car overheated. That's why we pulled over to the shoulder. We didn't block traffic or anything like that, anything wrong."

By this time the two young men had walked a hundred or so meters and had crossed a railway bridge. The police raised their rifles and shouted: "Get back here! Come back!" Gerardo told me that the two young men stopped while the police aimed their rifles at them and shouted for them to return. "So those guys took off running," he told me, "One of the police chased after them for about fifty meters, but couldn't catch them; they left."

The police kept interrogating the three men, asking repeatedly who they were, where they were going, what their jobs were, and how they knew the two young men. Gerardo Tzompaxtle told the officer interrogating him that he ran a small store. Both he and his brother are the owners of a small corner store in Astacinga, where they both live. Gerardo also grows corn, two different kinds of beans, and peas. The police did not believe him. (Gerardo told me that later the police searched their store as well as both his and his brother's houses.) The police—and later many of the reporters and columnists who commented on the case—said that it was impossible for an indigenous man such as Gerardo to have a 2001 Volkswagen Jetta. So they said: The brothers aren't small farmers and businessmen; they are criminals. "So that's where discrimination comes into play, don't you think?" Gerardo asked.

I asked Gerardo if at any point the police showed him anything written in the datebook that they said they found in the trunk. "There were some documents in there," he told me. "They said they were . . . like an analysis about whether or not that guy Obrador could win the elections." I asked him about the "propaganda documents alluding to the EPR" that the PGR claimed to have found in his car. "They got that off the internet and put it in the case file," he told me.

The police held the three men there on the highway shoulder for about two hours. The police then took them to a police station in Rio Blanco, a bit outside of Orizaba. There the police stripped the men of their wallets, belts, and watches and documented the belongings. The police tried to document the two cellular phones found in the young men's backpacks as belonging to Gerardo. At the station in Río Blanco the police once again separated the three men and interrogated them.

"That's where they started interrogating us again," Gerardo said, "asking who we were, whom were we going to kidnap, whom were we going to murder. Then a bunch of luxury cars arrived. A lot of people. I would guess that they were feds, the ones who interrogated me. They didn't really give us a chance to rest. One would come in, then another, and all of them asking us who we were, what we were doing, if we were kidnappers or guerrillas. That's when they started throwing that term at us. After a while, it would have been about seven at night, they brought us out of the police station and took us to the offices of the PGR in Orizaba. They put us in a little jail, a room. Around eight at night they started interrogating us again, whether we were guerrillas and all that. The local police were freaked out. They asked us what we were up to, because outside the Army had shut off all the streets. Then the police asked us where we had been planning to hide the stash of weapons they found. It was just a lie they made up. We didn't have any guns. I've never even shot a gun. They said that they had found a whole bunch of guns on us, but that was pure lies."

Their families found a lawyer who went to the PGR offices in Orizaba, but the police would not let the lawyer speak with the three men. That Friday, January 13, the men spent the entire day closed up in the room. A tall, civilian-dressed man made them take off their shirts and pants and face the wall stretching out their arms. He examined the soles of their feet, their calf muscles and their shoulders. Then he said: "You can walk a good while with that backpack, no? Yep, these are guerrillas."

Around dawn on Saturday, January 14, the police took the men out of the cell where they had been held since Thursday evening, with their wrists and ankles cuffed, and led them to a vehicle with ten armed agents. They sped through all the tollbooths. "We didn't even know where they were taking us," Gerardo told me. They arrived at a SIEDO office building in Mexico City around seven in the morning. They were made to walk down "a gauntlet of armed and masked agents. They told us that now they were going to make us talk, that they were going to beat the shit out of us. They mocked us."

The police again separated the three men and again interrogated them. Around noon each of the three men was made to give a statement to the federal prosecutor with four armed agents from the Federal Investigative Agency (AFI) guarding them: two in front and two behind.

"So you're the famous Rafael?" the federal prosecutor asked Gerardo.

"No."

"Rafael," he repeated, "Andrés's pseudonym."

"I don't know what you're talking about."

"Where is he?" the prosecutor asked in a mocking tone.

"I haven't seen my brother Andrés in years. I would lie if I told you where he was. I haven't seen him in years. I might not even recognize him if I were to see him."

"Well, today you guys are fucked and it's Rafael's fault. Your brother, we had him. We had him and he slipped out of our hands."

"Um, I don't know. . . . "

"You guys are going to do some years inside. You're going to spend some years in prison."

"And that asshole laughed, that federal prosecutor," Gerardo Tzompaxtle told me.

On October 16, 2008, two years and nine months after their arrest, Gerardo and Jorge Tzompaxtle Tecpile and Gustavo Robles López were acquitted of all counts of organized crime and kidnapping due to lack of evidence. They were found guilty of attempted bribery, a crime that carries a three-month sentence. At ten that night the three men walked free.[2]

TZOMPAXTLE AND NUBE

IN HIS WRITTEN TESTIMONY ANDRÉS Tzompaxtle refers to his wife and children as "Nube" (cloud): "When I had been pinned down my closest loved ones came into my mind and memories of testimonies of various compañeros and other social activists about what falling into enemy hands entails. I [said to myself], today it is my turn, my loved ones may never see me again, I will do everything to resist, and if I must die I hope not to betray anyone, and you, Nube, take care of the treasure you hold in your hands."

Tzompaxtle spoke about them several times during our interviews, especially in relation to the house in Acapulco that he never revealed to his torturers. "I would never have given up that house. It became the symbol, or I converted it into the symbol, of my life. I traded that house for my life," he told me. The house fell into enemy hands due to the carelessness of his compañeros and it was there, in that house, that military intelligence agents found the photograph.

After some time I asked Tzompaxtle if I could speak with Nube, interview her about her experiences, about what she lived through during those months when he was disappeared. He told me that he did not know if that would be possible, but that he would think about it and consult with Nube. When we saw each other a few months later, he told me that I would not be able to talk directly with Nube, but that I could give him some written questions and he would bring me her answers. I made another proposal: What if I lent Tzompaxtle my digital voice recorder, wrote down a few questions that he could ask her, and he could record their conversation and bring me back the recorder with their interview? He said yes.

I tore a sheet out of my notebook and quickly wrote down some questions. I asked if Nube would mind telling me a bit about her childhood, her adolescence, her decision to join the armed struggle, how she met and fell in love with Tzompaxtle, how she found out about his disappearance, and what she lived through during those months, how she found out that her husband had escaped, and what she felt upon being reunited with him. I told Tzompaxtle that my questions were only guides to begin a conversation, and that he should ask any questions he wanted to, and that she should feel free to speak about anything she might want to share. I told him that I hoped to listen to her speak about her life, her thoughts, and her experiences having her compañero—husband and father of her children—disappeared and then reappeared. I took out my voice recorder and gave it to him.

I was aware of the theoretical and practical risks of my proposal. Would Nube modify her answers speaking to her husband and in the presence of a voice recorder? Yes, the person who listens always impacts the person who speaks and their manner of speaking. By the same logic, she would modify her responses speaking directly to me. Could Tzompaxtle manipulate her responses or even find some other woman to say whatever he wanted her to say? Theoretically, yes. But, on the one hand, if I so mistrusted Tzompaxtle I wouldn't be doing this. On the other hand, the core, bare-bones, essential truth of a story can be heard in the voice just as it can be seen in the face of the one who speaks. There may be distortions, evasions, silences, missing information, but the emotional truth of having lived through the disappearance of one's husband would be present. Evidence of this could be found in any of the numerous meetings or protests organized by family members of the disappeared. I would not be able to see Nube's face, but I trusted that I would hear a bit of her truth in the recording of her voice. And after listening to the recording, that trust only deepened. When Nube doesn't want to speak about something she tells Tzompaxtle so directly, just as he did with me. Such honesty inspires trust, as do the emotions in the voice. I felt that I could hear Nube smiling when she spoke of being a small child in the country and seeing newborn birds in their nest. I could hear her anger when she spoke of growing up hungry, working for poverty wages, suffering from racism. I heard the certainty and anger in her voice when Tzompaxtle asked her if she ever thought that he could betray her during torture and she fired the word "*¡Jamás!*" (Never!) like a bullet. I heard her voice break, repeatedly, when she tried to describe the pain she felt when her compañero was disappeared.

What follows is, with minimal editing, the interview between Tzompaxtle and his wife Nube.

Nube: My childhood . . . my childhood was two things: the negative and the positive, that is the beautiful. Hunger, for example, is not beautiful because you suffer humiliations. My childhood. What I remember is that it was really fun for me, happy: running, free, always free, always running. Or when my mom—more than anyone, her—taught me to work in the house, I was happy then. But on the other hand, when I didn't have my mom then there wasn't any happiness. And being hungry, and barefoot. But more than clothing, things to wear, it was food that worried us. It wasn't that I was well-dressed. Hunger, it isn't very . . . what more can I say about that? Hunger is hunger. It doesn't matter if you are barefoot, it doesn't matter if you only have one dress, if your stomach has something . . . if you have something to eat.

Happiness was running, being with my mom, with my brothers. Living, among other things, it was the happiness that I had. Beyond that, my happiness was the necessity of helping someone. Perhaps carrying water, because they'd give you a piece of bread or something to eat.

Tzompaxtle: When you speak of playing, what did you play? What was play for you? Besides running and jumping.

Nube: What other kinds of playing? I didn't have dolls, but something that the indigenous people teach is that you don't necessarily have to have a doll. Do you know what we played with, what they taught me to play with? For example, when we had corn cobs, my mom taught me that a cob could be a baby. They gave you the corn cob half-wrapped in a piece of a rag and they told you: "See, this is your doll." But in the end, it wasn't a doll; it was a corn cob. We played with those. My cousins and I. We played a lot together.

We also played "mealtime." We cut some big leaves and those were our plates. We grabbed some rocks and those were our pieces of bread. We pretended that it was food. During the fruit seasons we played with the fruit, with whatever there was. When you don't have anything, then what are you going to play with? We had some animals, though not many. That was also fun: when the little lambs are born it is really cool. It excites you because they are being born, you see it differently. It filled me with joy. Even today when I see something tiny that has just been born, it is a little creature that is alive and it makes me . . . I don't know. Those are the things I played with.

Tzompaxtle: Did you see it as a pet?

Nube: Well, to be honest, I didn't know what a pet was.

Tzompaxtle: How did you see it?

Nube: Well, it was more like part of the family. A little animal that we also need for protection, because it would watch over us at night. I just knew that it was a little animal, that we had a puppy there, in the house, like a part of the family.

Tzompaxtle: What feelings, or sensibilities, did it create in you?

Nube: Sensibility . . . joy. So much, a lot . . . It isn't the same as having a doll. You are playing with something that is alive. It isn't the same as a stuffed animal that they buy for some rich kid, for a child that has the possibility to have things, as something that is alive, no? And that is . . . for me it was always exciting. I wouldn't trade it for anything in the world.

Tzompaxtle: What other things were a part of your childhood?

Nube: Clouds, stars. Things that I don't . . .

Tzompaxtle: Were those your only favorite animals?

Nube: There were a lot of things. In the country, even though you live in squalor, there is something more. For example, I was fascinated by, you know what? Little birds. I'd go look for their nests to see how they are born. There are little eggs there, and if you go back in fifteen or twenty days they'll have hatched. That is really neat. You know what else? I'd look for tiny worms and I'd take them to the nests. The baby birds open their little beaks like this and then I'd give them something to eat. That was fun to me.

The tree . . . to grow amidst trees. It's not the same seeing cars and buildings without trees. Like they are life-less things. That's how the big cities are these days, more buildings than trees. I'd stick with what I experienced as a girl. All of it. Except the hunger.

Tzompaxtle: What else did you learn as a child? What work did you learn how to do?

Nube: In the country, well, to work the *milpa*,* cut weeds, split wood, gather wood, to grind using the *metate*.** I'm not saying that I do it well, but more or less I know how to prepare the corn for making tortillas the following day.

Tzompaxtle: Okay. Anything else?

Nube: Well, when I went to school, more than anything I liked the opportunity that I had. My brothers went, but they only learned a bit to read and write. My little brother went up to first grade. My brother who died didn't really go to school. They taught me games. They taught me to defend myself during that part of my childhood.

---

* Fields combining corn, beans, and other vegetables such as chilies or squash.
** A usually rectangular stone mortar.

Tzompaxtle: What did you feel at school? What did school mean to you?

Nube: To learn. To know more things. You know what? What intrigued me were big cities. I always said, "I want to go there, see how people live, maybe they live better." I was always curious, since I was a girl. I'd say: "I don't want to stay here. I want . . . " It's absurd. As a girl, when I was eleven years old, I learned to give injections. What made me so sad was that there were no doctors. But people came to know that I could give injections and they all brought me their babies. Sometimes they woke me up at night, or when it was raining. Even today it makes me so sad, I don't know. Perhaps because my mom was always sick, but that, that feeling . I don't want to go there because it hurts. It hurts just remembering it. No. I don't want to.

Tzompaxtle: What did learning to read, or learning to speak another language mean to you?

Nube: At school they forced things on you that . . . Well, learning is good. To read and write, no? But the things that they started forcing us to do . . . Your language. They told you not to speak your language, that you had to speak Spanish. It was confusing. I mean, now I say "confusing" but then I didn't even know what "confusing" meant. The first teacher I had didn't speak Náhuatl, I don't think. So it was hard for us, well it was hard work for me personally, to know what the teacher was saying.

Later, when you start learning to read and the book is not in your language, you don't even know what the book is saying. You don't understand. It is hard for an indigenous person, for someone who doesn't speak that language. And the questions . . . you have to answer them in Spanish.

That part was really hard for me. I know that as I learned it was like a kind of awakening. And moreover, in the books we saw how people lived in the cities. That's why I had the curiosity to see how they are, how people live there. Later I realized that the things the books said isn't what it's like to live there. You see it differently. There is a big difference. For example, when you read a book and then see how the people in your town live, how others live, and you see the inequality. In the book you see kids playing, going to school, and they have shoes and you see that you're barefoot.

Tzompaxtle: If you were to tell something else from those same years that marked your life, sad or happy . . .

Nube: I wish that my mom had always been with us. That she never . . . Every time she had to leave to work I wanted to go with her. I didn't want to stay with my grandfather. He also loved me, but I wanted to be with her. I didn't want her to leave. I think that is something that always marked me.

Tzompaxtle: Her absence?

Nube: Yes. She would leave to work for two or three months, depending on the season and the harvests. Whether it was coffee or sugarcane.

Tzompaxtle: So, she emigrated to . . .

Nube: Uh-huh.

Tzompaxtle: Filling the roles of . . .

Nube: Of father and mother. My mom was the one who taught me to sharpen a machete, to work in the *milpa*. More than my grandmother, it was my mom. That is what marked me. I'll never forget that she wasn't there. But it also made me so happy when she came back. She'd bring

food. We liked her to bring us peanuts or some fruit that
was different from what grew around us. I waited for her
with so much joy. I think all of that is what I'll never forget.

Tzompaxtle: And, after your childhood, what
happened?

Nube: I finished elementary school. I went to a board-
ing school. I cried so much when I went there.

Tzompaxtle: And what happened after that?

Nube: Before finishing elementary school, in the fifth
grade, I went to the city with a school administrator (*ecónoma*). We called her teacher, but she wasn't really a teacher.
She was someone who prepared food for us to eat at the
school. But we also learned from her, and she would put us
to work. We'd go out to gather firewood in groups. They'd
make us tutor others, make the beds, bathe, sweep. What
else? They also formed commissions and sent us to make
tortillas (like governors, who say they form commissions,
no?). In our commission we'd make tortillas and go bring
water. Other groups cleaned, for example. Some would
grind the *nixtamal** and others would make the tortillas.
This wasn't always hard; it had its fun side too. After a
time, I liked being there. The administrator (*ecónoma*) said
that she had been to Mexico City. One day I told her: "Ay,
how exciting, I want to go, I want to visit that city." And
she said to me: "Well then, you go and work there." And
so I went with her to the city. I think I just worked for the
two months of vacation; I worked with some people that
she knew; she sent me to them. No, it was like twenty days.
And, what did I do? I'd make the beds—the woman of

---

*   Mixture of ground corn, water, and lime used in making tortillas.

the house taught me how—but I didn't understand much because I didn't speak Spanish. I spoke Náhuatl. I barely spoke my own language and that woman—I think her name was Graciela, or if she is still alive, her name is Graciela—would teach me things, saying: "No, this is called this. You say it like this and you talk this way. Call things by their names."

I cried a lot, every night. I wanted to see my mom. I closed my eyes and I couldn't see her. Even though I was used to getting through days at a time without her. Mountains, cities, and highways separated us. I couldn't see her. Moreover, I couldn't see any of my people, people from my *pueblo*. But I had also said that I wasn't going to go back, that I wanted to go to the city and work and learn. But, unfortunately, when I wanted to study no one gave me permission. They told me: "No, you have to work. You don't have any time." That was unjust to me. I started losing my initiative, but I enrolled to study first aid and nursing on Sundays.

I met some women friends who told me, "There is a school where I study on Sundays; it is really cool and you learn, they teach you." I liked it, and since I already knew how to give injections, I wanted to learn how to put an IV in someone. It was also really excellent for me because I also wanted to continue studying middle school. They accepted me having only completed elementary school to start learning first aid and nursing. I really liked that. I mean, I wanted to learn and they accepted me. I started and I completed the course. Afterward I started working in what I enjoyed: I became a caretaker for children and the elderly, even though the pay was only so-so. Before that, for example, when I didn't know how to do anything, there was a lot of humiliation. When you work as a domestic worker they humiliate you.

There are good people, but you don't always get to deal with them. People humiliate you for being indigenous and because you don't understand what they are telling you. That is also humiliating. Or they call you "Indian." That didn't offend me, being Indian. On the contrary, I'm very proud to be Indian. If someone says that to me, thanks, I don't forget my roots.

But I saw that there were always injustices. There was no equality. All that stuff they tell you on television, that everyone is good: that didn't exist. That isn't true. It hurts to see the hunger, the injustices. And so I realized that if you live in a big city it isn't true that you live better. Cities aren't like they tell you in the books. You don't see everyone happy and wearing shoes. You see children in the street. Children without food to eat. Children who are not well at all.

And you ask: why? I asked myself that. Why is this like it is if I'm living in the big city? Why is there still hunger? If people go hungry there, it's because there aren't jobs. Even though supposedly that shouldn't happen in the city. On the news they say that everyone has jobs, everyone eats well, everyone lives well, and you go out into the street and see that it isn't true, that it's a big lie. You see how they humiliate people. I remember working in a store where they sent a man to prison for stealing. He was taking something to eat because he didn't have any money. And the woman who did the accounting would tell him: "At the end of the week when the boss pays you, then you can pay me what you owe." And they would do that, but the boss caught him and sent him to prison saying that he was stealing. But he wasn't stealing, he was going to pay.

So you want to tell him: "If he was going to pay you he wasn't stealing." But the owner didn't want to lose one cent. They don't care if your family is dying of hunger. No. They have to make money every day. They don't have any reason to lose their interests. I was indignant to see that and even though the other workers said, "Look, we'll put the money together amongst us and pay you." Despite all that, the owner sent him to prison. I don't know how many years they gave him, but I do know that he went to prison.

That is not okay. How do you explain it when someone steals more and goes free, or steals much more and gets off with a good lawyer? That's how I learned the way that lawyers work, how they bribe people.

Things aren't like they tell us in stories or like the government officials say: "Nothing's wrong, nothing's happening." You are indignant. You start to feel. . . it's a kind of powerlessness, you don't know what to do, whom to tell. We all know it but nobody wants to stick their hands in the fire, nobody wants to say: "This is wrong." That's when I woke up. You start looking for, I don't know, for what you should do. I mean, if you have a bit of feeling and humanism. I met some people who weren't either really rich or really poor, but who had a degree of preparation, and I followed them. They also started to say: "This is wrong, this shouldn't be like this, this shouldn't be happening. How is it possible for people to live like this?" And so you say: "You know, I have the same feelings, I think the same way." And that is what leads you to . . . I mean, you get indignant. And so you start getting involved, no?

Tzompaxtle: Yeah . . . It is really a matter of lived experience . . .

Nube: Of what one sees. No one can tell you: "Hey, come with me, do this." You think for yourself: "This can't go on." If you don't want to act, no one can force you to do so. It is something so real, the indignation, seeing mistreatment, the indignation of seeing how a handful live better. That is not just.

You say: "How is it possible that no one does anything and everything stays the same, the streets, the poverty, the hunger, the barefoot children in the mountains?" I mean, I lived that, I know what hunger is: You don't eat and you go to sleep without having eaten. These days they say that a pregnant woman should be well nourished, that she should take certain things, but that is marketing, nothing else. It is like saying: "Look at all we the government officials do, we give you all this, but you all just don't take it." But that is not true, not everyone has such things within their reach. Otherwise no one would be poor. Everyone would be okay, would have work. No. Something is wrong. Something isn't right or isn't working.

Tzompaxtle: And how were you able get involved in the struggle?

Nube: How? Well, because you meet people who think the same way, they have a bit of feelings, they have . . . how to say this with different words? They have some dignity, values. There are people who after everything, after the hunger, destitution, cold, after all that, keep thinking like you do, but they don't do anything. No one does anything. Everything stays the same. When you meet these people who think like you do and they have some sensitivity, you say: "Well, here they think like I do; I'm not the only one." You realize that there are more and more people.

Tzompaxtle: What did it mean to you to make the decision, to change your life? Because joining the struggle meant breaking with a way of life.

Nube: Let's say a tradition.

Tzompaxtle: What did you feel? What emotions, fears, doubts? What . . . ? What challenges did you face, especially as a woman?

Nube: Doubts? No. Because I knew what I wanted. Fear? Well, I think all humans feel some fear. I don't think anyone isn't afraid. When you come into this and you learn that someone was tortured, even if they haven't done anything, but they get tortured . . .

But maybe it is worth it being here. Because living another thousand years like this, like always, without doing anything? There is no justice in that.

It upsets me seeing how other children suffer like I did. It upsets me to see that. I don't like it. I'd like to see a world that is more . . . more wonderful. A world without hunger, where we'd all see each other as equals, where the wealthy wouldn't just accumulate their money only thinking of themselves. A more just world. That people would have better salaries, that they could live better. But no one does this, no? I mean, the businesspeople. They don't like losing. They constantly amass their money and they don't care if you have a family, if you have something to eat, if you have clothes to wear. We are a Third World country. There are members of Congress who say: "You know, I guess people just like living like that." I've always heard that.

Another thing that marked me when I entered into the struggle was when I worked in a house—the third one—and one Christmas they told the story that they called "the Christmas spirit." They told their children and their employees why poor people don't have any money. "They don't have any money because they spend it. They spend it all; they spend everything they earn." And that people who are poor should thank them because they give us jobs. Because that is how God wanted it to be. That is what they said. More than the others, I remember that their daughter really marked me. I remember how she answered them: "Mom, that's not true. My dad pays his employees very little, and they can't live on the small amount of money they earn. They can't afford to study, a car, or pay rent. We do have a big house, we have servants, we have nannies, we have people who take care of us. But do you think dad's employees could have a house just like ours?" And I remember how her mother got angry and told her, "Shut up or I'll send you to your room! You shouldn't be talking, remember that all the servants are here."

And so you think: "They think they are saviors because the give people jobs. But since we don't know how to save, we spend everything. But how much do they pay you? How much do you make? And that's when you start to really dislike like rich people. And they believe that we don't even think, that we are worthless, and that's another humiliation. That's when you get more indignant and you think, "I can't be hearing this, they can't be saying this in front of me. And I can't do anything. I can't say that their daughter is telling the truth, that they pay me a pittance."

You keep quiet even though you don't like it. If her daughter is confronting her and telling her the truth, it's because it is true. She just told the pure truth, but the woman says: "No. God sent us to take care of them, to give them work." And so you ask yourself: what work? They exploit you, and either they don't pay you or they pay you a pittance. And on top of it all they want you to live better or to save up. But how can you save if you can't even go to the supermarket to buy what you need with what they pay you?

You can't live like that. A person can't live like that. It is impossible.

Tzompaxtle: How old was the daughter?

Nube: She was . . . sixteen.

Tzompaxlte: Once you were inside, how did you feel?

Nube: Awful. I wanted to run and tell her that, I wanted to tell her that she was a . . .

Tzompaxtle: No, I mean, once you were inside . . . [the guerrilla organization].

Nube: Ah, here. How did I feel? Good, and I saw things . . . I saw that there is equality, that it doesn't matter if you're a woman or man. They treat you the same way. They share things. If food is short, everyone eats the same amount. That is what unites you, no? That is what unites you as a human, as a living being, who must protect itself from many things. Not just protect people and protect children from hunger, but also to take care of nature, not destroy it, plunder it, or sell it. What you learn as a child: that one shouldn't exploit the land too much. And then you see that the businessman just comes to exploit human beings, and our lands . . .

There is enough money for the *pueblos* to live better.

But no . . . they plunder it. They bring Chinese, gringo, and Canadian corporations.

[It seems as if the recording pauses here. When it continues, Nube is talking about falling in love.]

Nube: Falling in love is having children, it is part of life. Well, that's how I see it: It is part of who we are. It's amazing when you meet someone who thinks like you do. It makes you feel good. And if it's also a person who reads, who doesn't smoke, who isn't a drunk. Since I was a girl I always thought that I'd never be able to marry a drunk, nor an abusive husband, whether physically or mentally abusive. I believe that my ancestors heard me. With couples there are always difficulties, but that doesn't mean that I don't love my partner, or the person I live with. I could have lived without it, but it happened and it is . . . it can't be denied. Here we are.

Tzompaxtle: How did they tell you?

Nube: That I had to pack my things, that I had to go. I didn't know what had happened. They didn't tell me right at that moment. I could sense that something had happened, but I didn't know what.

When they tell you: "Let's go, come on, you have to leave from there," you know that something could have happened. Or when you ask where the person is and they answer: "He's over there," or "He's fine." And you're there, unable to do anything.

You already know what can happen: They can disappear you, kill you, torture you. And it isn't just you who knows it, everyone knows it. And even though you're conscious that it can happen at any time, no one wants it to.

That is what came into my mind. If something happened to him, I can't give up. I can't quit, nor feel ashamed: I can't tell the government: "I regret it."

Whoever had my husband in their hands was already torturing him, because that is what happens. When someone falls into enemy hands, there is always torture, beatings, even more so when the person is disappeared. If they "appear" the person one or two days later, then it is easier because you know that the person could be in prison. I said to myself: "He has to appear, and if they arrest him, then let him be judged for what he has done. What is his crime? Well, what he did." But he was disappeared and they never arrested him. The pain is so, so intense. It hurt, but I never thought about giving up the struggle. I never thought about leaving. Because that would be saying that the people who have him in their hands are right.

You think that he's already gone through something, and you really want them to present him, to judge him, as it should be. Those are the prisoner's rights. If they have him, they should say, "We have him here."

I don't see that he's done anything that bad; he didn't kill anyone, he didn't do anything. It is not bad to protest, to think about others. It means that you have values, dignity, but not everyone does. The majority of people do things, but to benefit themselves. That hurts. And maybe it begins to scar, and those scars remain always. You'll never be able to forget them. Can you heal 100 percent? No. You always think that it will happen again.

I don't regret anything. We are not—as they call

us—criminals. We are not part of organized crime. No. We are here for a reason. For equality, no?

Tzompaxtle: What did you live through during the months when he was disappeared? What did you feel?

Nube: With the pain of thinking that I'd never see him again. It is a terrible thing. I wouldn't wish it on anyone. No . . . there are no words for it . . . I don't know how to say it because it is something that hurts too much, not knowing where he is, or how he is. You can't sleep. You can't rest. You are always thinking about the same thing. In every instant. It is inexplicable to me. It would have been so different to have known that he was in prison, because then you wait for him to be judged and sentenced.

I always said to myself: "I won't give up until I find him, or they give him back, at least his body, until they tell me what they did to him, where he is." Because I felt that he was still alive, that he hadn't left. I always said to myself: "If I were born again, raised again, I wouldn't change, I would still be here. I would do the same thing." It is the same as when you have to decide. They ask you: "Are you in or out? There's no problem if you leave. It is your right." You respond: "I can't. If I leave, I surrender. He wouldn't like that. No. I have to fight."

I always felt that one day I would find him. But I also thought at times about death: "If you are dead, I can't leave, I'll stay here. I'll know how to survive it all. To survive this. But I know that you are alive and you'll be back. I'll find you. I don't know how many years it will take."

Sometimes books say: "He was disappeared and reappeared so many years later" or "they had him in such and such a place, they tortured him, he broke out and escaped."

I felt that he was alive. The pain is so strong. It is inexplicable. No. I don't know how to say it . . . What else can I say?

Tzompaxtle: How did the organization address the issue of your children? I suppose that the children didn't understand an explanation. What was it like with them?

Nube: Sad. I didn't know what to tell them. At times they'd say to me: "And dad?" And I would tell them, dad is alive and he'll be back any time now. That he would be . . . that we'd have to see him again and hug him and feel him and . . . I always said to myself: "He is very strong, it doesn't matter how they have him, it doesn't matter, he'll make it through." And to him: "You are strong. I don't know how you are, nor where you are. You have to endure. You have to resist. It sounds cruel, but it doesn't matter if they torture you, you have to endure. You can't let us down."

I never believed he was dead. Only once did I tell myself: "If he is dead I want his body. I want them to give me his body and then I'll rest. I wouldn't have to look for him, I'd know that they killed him." But I felt that it wasn't so. On the news, Ángel Aguirre said that he . . . that they had him, that the Army had him. They couldn't kill him because . . . they had him. Although I think Aguirre said that he made a mistake, that he didn't know. But he did, he did know. They all know what they do.

That spirit, that feeling that he was alive—"I don't know how or when or at what time, but one day I'll see him again"—that hope never died. I'd tell my children: "I don't know when, in how many years, I don't know, ten, fifteen, but you will see your dad again." I think that children always understand what you tell them, what you transmit to them. I remember that my daughter would tell me: "Dad's coming; he's coming back." So I think that in all that we weren't wrong. Here we are, and that is what counts: our family.

Tzompaxtle: And what feeling hit you when you found out or when they told you that he had appeared, that he had returned? How did you imagine he'd be? The same? Worse? Did you ever think that he would change and betray his ideals?

Nube: Never! Knowing him, never. He can't betray his ideals. Never.

Tzompaxtle: But he was being tortured.

Nube: It doesn't matter. When you know someone well enough, no . . .

Tzompaxtle: What are his traits?

Nube: His nobility, his lack of vanity, his humbleness. His feelings. I don't think that could have changed. What could he have done? Sold out? I don't think so. Because there were comments to that effect, that if they had him alive, that could have happened. He could have betrayed us. But I always said no, with absolute certainty. Before falling into betrayal he would have preferred to die. But not betray. He wasn't born to be a traitor. On the contrary, in that case none of what we believe, what we do, what he has always been would make any sense.

Tzompaxtle: What feelings remain after all that, on finding out that he has returned? What is the first thing you think, or the first thing you tell him?

Nube: To see him, hold him, and tell him that I missed him so much.

Tzompaxtle: What shape was he in when you saw him? What did they tell you at first?

Nube: They told me that he was in really bad shape, that the Army had done nearly everything to him. And that there was some risk that he could have betrayed. Being here was a really big risk, the compañeros said. They weren't certain that he had remained a man faithful Commander to the struggle. Faithful to what we do and what we love. I always told them that he would always remain loyal to the struggle. But they said it was possible that the Army had let him out.

I understood that it would have taken a lot of imagination to invent what he told, for what he said had happened to him; that's why he was thin, too thin. The only thing he did was cry. He had a feeling . . . he never denied the struggle. But he did feel pain, I don't know how to explain it. Just remembering it is . . . going back. What they did to him is despicable, it is . . . I think it is inhuman. When someone falls into their hands . . . it is outrageous. As a human being it is offensive to see a person taken to that point. But you say: "He is alive, he is here." That is what you value most. That is what matters. What happened, it happened. It is irremediable. They already tortured him. We can't turn back the clock. We just have to struggle so that it doesn't happened to him again nor to anyone else ever. It doesn't matter who they may be. It doesn't matter what race they may be or where they may be from. People should have feelings, they should become outraged by what happens to people. And I'm not inventing anything. You see it in the news, hear it on the radio, see it on television, or in the newspaper. It shouldn't happen to anyone. Anyone.

When they captured him they should have openly

acknowledged it, not tortured him. Because, in the end, we are all . . . we are all equal. I don't know what becomes of the ones who torture, I don't even know why they do it. They really are slaves to a system, no? That's what I think. We are free, we want to be free. But they won't let us be free. And our freedom is the struggle, so that we can all be equals.

Tzompaxtle: Why do you think they doubted? What led them to doubt, or what was the main idea of the doubt the *compañeros* had concerning him? What did they base their doubt in?

Nube: Well, I don't know. If they doubted, it could be because . . . many things went through their heads. I don't know. I won't answer that. I don't want to answer. I don't want to.

[Someone turns off the voice recorder.]

THE DISAPPEARED

ON THURSDAY, MAY 10, 2012, the mothers marched through the streets of Mexico City.[1] Their children were disappeared and the authorities—or at least that's what they call them—have done nothing to look for them. Many of the mothers, and also sisters, daughters, and nieces, carried signs with the names and photographs of the disappeared. Some of the signs also showed the dates, times, and places of the abductions. On many of these signs could be read the name of the police or military unit that disappeared their children. How did the mothers know who took their children? Because they witnessed the abductions, or because they themselves investigated. There they went, floating in the air, advancing along Reforma Avenue, from the Monument to the Revolution to the Angel of Independence, the absent children, their absent case files, their absent investigations. The names, faces, and brief details of the horror that took them, all printed on poster board and held aloft by the women who marched that day. One can count the names. One can measure the distance they walked. One can view the photographs and the videos reporters and activists took. One can hear the recordings of their chants. But the pain . . .

When I realized that all these disappearances were not enmeshed in some irremediable uncertainty, when I understood that there were solid investigations, that the absent case files were held up there for all to see, I approached a woman near me in the march. I read the sign she carried and wrote down what it said in my notebook: "Juan Manuel Bustamante Morales; thirty-four years old; from Ciudad Juárez; forcibly disappeared; culprit: Federal Police; place: Veracruz Port." María Luisa, from Chihuahua, told me that she filed charges against the police, but the authorities treated her with indifference. When she went back to review the case file, the investigation was stalled. When the people suffering the horror "are everyday people," she said, the government "doesn't do a thing."

I thanked her for speaking with me and stood for a moment, watching the march advance. I looked at all the absences in the air. I noticed that a number of the signs all had the same last name. I started walking again, and wrote down in my notebook the information on another of the signs: "Guadalupe Muñoz Veleta; thirty-six years old; forcibly disappeared; culprit: Municipal Police and Federal Police; June 19, 2011; Anáhuac, Chihuahua." I approached the young woman carrying the sign and asked her name and age: Diana, sixteen. I asked about the sign she was carrying, and she said: "On Father's Day they were having a family gathering and federal and municipal police busted into the house and took Guadalupe along with seven other members of the family."

The woman who walked beside Diana, the wife of one of the disappeared men, told me: "It is very clear that the authorities don't want to help. Despite the fact that our family has given them evidence and information for the investigation, there aren't doing anything. We have identified the police officers responsible, and they are all still on the job. Basically, we're destroyed. Eight members of the same family disappeared. Pretty much just us women are left. We are struggling to raise our children. Without a death certificate we can't request economic support. My daughters ask me, 'Where's my dad?' and I don't know what to tell them." One of her daughters, six years old, was there that night and saw everything. "My four-year-old asks me, 'Where's my dad? I miss him so much,' and I don't know what to tell him," she said, and wept. I closed my notebook. I offered her my hand, she offered hers; I held it for a moment, a clumsy attempt to offer and give a gentle hug while marching, and then kept walking with them.

Some time later, a journalist from Chihuahua who had interviewed members of the family told me this: The family was in their house, celebrating Father's Day. Outside, a group of men were bothering them. The family, after trying to speak with the men, called the police. Officers were slow to arrive, and when they did, they simply went to talk and hang out with the men who were bothering the family. One of the young men in the house jumped inside the police patrol car, which had the keys still in the ignition. The young man revved the engine, drove a few meters and stopped. He then got out of the car and screamed at the cops to leave: "You cops are fucking worthless" ("*no sirven para ni madres*"). The police, furious, made a phone call. An armed convoy arrived and together with the police they abducted eight men from the family. They are all still disappeared.

The statistics hurt. The numbers cut and burn. Subtle violence that razes what it seeks to convey. You pronounce the number—25,276—and it is an even surface. The pain is compressed and removed from sight. But it is not extinguished. It remains, and it boils there, beneath the surface. The statistic buries you. No number can face the pain of not knowing where the person you love is, the pain of finding machines of impunity operating in every public office, every telephone, every newspaper, every street corner.

But there is no exit. The statistic wounds, but you still pronounce the number: 25,276. At least 25,276 people were forcibly disappeared between December 2006 and July 2012.[2] This number is an official statistic from office of the Federal Attorney General (PGR) and the state prosecutors from all thirty-one states and the Federal District.[3] It is an impossible number. It cannot sustain the weight of the pain it carries and conceals. It is a number that must itself cause pain, its very impossibility and violence must break the comfort with which one can pronounce it. Rage. It should provoke rage. Between January 1995 and December 1996 two human rights organizations counted thirty-eight cases of forced disappearance in Mexico.[4] From thirty-eight in two years to 25,276 cases in five and a half years. From an "average" of nineteen a year to one of 4,595 cases a year. Not cases. They are not cases. They are people. The numbers, if they are to be useful at all, must hurt.

As part of his 2000 presidential campaign, Vicente Fox of the National Action Party (PAN) said that, if elected, he would form a "truth commission" to investigate the massacres of October 2, 1968, and June 10, 1971, as well as other "state crimes" of the 1970s and 1980s. He did not include in his promise the massacres of June 28, 1995, December 22, 1997, or June 7, 1998, nor other "state crimes" of the 1990s. Fox won the 2000 elections and became the first non-PRI president to take office in seventy-one years. In January 2002, Fox established the Special Prosecutor for Social and Political Movements of the Past. On December 15, 2005, the Special Prosecutor delivered its report to the PGR. The report was titled: "Report: May It Never Happen Again!" (*Informe: ¡Qué no vuelva a suceder!*).[5] Eleven months later, the PGR posted online a modified version of the report titled: "Historic Report to Mexican Society 2006" (*Informe histórico a la sociedad Mexicana 2006*). This version lacked chapter fourteen of the original report, titled: "Conclusions and recommendations." Carlos Montemayor, in his essay "The Special Prosecutor," notes:

> [Chapter 14 is] where they analyzed the reasons the motivated rebellions and the structural violence that the rebellions responded to; where they described the unnecessary, excessive, and criminal use of force by the State and the seriousness of the fact that the State itself had committed crimes against humanity; and where they discussed the need to revise and change the institutional structure of the Army, for example the DN-II and the military code, that enable the Army's deployment in public security and police tasks; the chapter also proposed the imperative need for the State to reveal the fate of the people disappeared while in State custody and

the State's obligation to in whatever way possible repair the damage done to the victims.[6]

Montemayor describes other omissions from the PGR's published version of the report:

> They suppressed parts of other chapters and they changed the names of various crimes against humanity to qualify and minimize the Army's responsibility for the crimes committed by soldiers and officers. "Forced disappearance" was reclassified as "illegal deprivation of freedom."[7]

I asked José Gil Olmos from *Proceso* magazine if he thought there was a relation between Tzompaxtle's forced disappearance and the eruption of forced disappearances occurring across Mexico from 2007 up to the present. This was his response:

> There is something gravely serious with these types of testimonies. What we were able to show was that the same strategy used in the 1970s to eliminate the guerrillas is now used to benefit organized crime. It is as if what they learned in training they now apply differently and with completely different goals. But it is exactly the same thing. I mean, they are soldiers and police who at some point received training in that school, were taught to combat rebels, but after the rebels no longer posed the same threat, well, those soldiers and police now participate in organized crime and use what they learned in school for

their illegal business. That is, the practices are the same, but the objectives are different.

But I do not doubt that the people carrying out forced disappearances are soldiers and police. An example of this—and something related that can shed a bit of light on this—is that before, the people who charged you protection money were the Secretary of Commerce or the Tax Agency. They would show up to your business and charge you money in order to let you work. This happened to my father. That is, the tax collector showed up in person and said: "You're missing these documents; if you don't want us to shut you down, pay up."

Well, that same practice is now perpetrated by organized crime. They say something like, if you want to keep working, you want to keep your business, you'll have to pay us a cut. It is the same thing exactly, just with different people. With forced disappearance it is the same practice, but with different intentions. In the 1970s, it was the State attempting to suppress protest and rebellion, and in recent years it's the same State agents, but for personal benefit.

And that's why Rafael's case is so emblematic, because despite the suspicion around his escape and all that, what it showed you was that the same practices were still in use; they hadn't stopped. They were still in use against the guerrillas and now they are even more in use with organized crime. The thing is that in the "Dirty War," there were 1,500 disappeared people. Now we are talking about

26,000 or 27,000 officially. We're talking about the population of a town.

You know what? It's as if forced disappearance remained as a kind of traditional rite of the Mexican State.

After escaping, more than anything, Tzompaxtle wanted people to listen to him. It would seem as if very few people have. In his testimony, with all its silences and uncertainties and ruptures, we find the warning that was not heard, the knowledge that was never acknowledged.

We also find, staring into the mouth of hell, the will to escape.

ENDNOTES

THE JOURNALISTS

1. The repression continued. Within five years 42 more men had been murdered in relation to the Aguas Blanca Massacre. See, Carlos Montemayor's 2010 book *La violencia de Estado en México. Antes y después de 1968* (Mexico City: Debate, 2010), p. 192. For background on the formation of the EPR in Guerrero, see my profile of Gloria Arenas in *Mexico Unconquered: Chronicles of Power and Revolt* (San Francisco: City Lights, 2009), pp. 231–265.

2. See "Acuerdo del Tribunal Pleno de la Suprema Corte de Justicia de la Nación correspondiente al expediente 3/96," April, 23 1996; Maribel Gutiérrez, *Violencia en Guerrero* (Mexico City: La Jornada Ediciones, 1998), pp. 119–131; Gloria Leticia Díaz, "Cinco años de la matanza. Aguas Blancas: la pesadilla no termina," in *Proceso*, June 24, 2000; and for information on the Aguas Blancas massacre in English, see the Minnesota Advocates for Human Rights December 1995 report, "Massacre in Mexico: Killings and Cover-Up in the State of Guerrero."

3. Maribel Gutiérrez, *Violencia en Guerrero*, p. 223.

4. Jon Lee Anderson, *Guerrillas* (New York: Penguin Books, 2004), p. xi.

5. Guerrero state statistics for 1996 taken from the Encuesta Nacional de Alimentación y Nutrición en el Medio Rural.

6. Laura Castellaños, *México Armado. 1943–1981* (Mexico City: Ediciones Era, 2007), pp. 109–110, 113–114, 117–120; Marco Bellingeri, *Del agrarismo armado a la guerra de los pobres* (Mexico City: Ediciones Casa Juan Pablos, 2003), *1940–1974*, pp. 121,125, 133–134, 178. One of the most powerful books on Guerrero during those years is Carlos Montemayor's historical novel *Guerra en el Paraíso* (Mexico City: Debolsillo, 2009).

7. In April 1970, 25,000 soldiers were deployed in Guerrero, a third of the standing army. "The articulate Secretary of Defense, General Hermenegildo Cuenca Díaz, justified this mobilization by referring to the struggle against drug trafficking and the support for vacationers," Castellanos, *México armado*, p. 126.

8. Carlos Montemayor, *La guerrilla recurrente* (Mexico City: Debate, 2007), p. 13.

9. Ibid., p. 23.

10. Carlos Montemayor, *La violencia de Estado en México*, p. 182.

11. Salvador Corro, "En una sangrienta noche de terror, las fuerzas del EPR destruyen el mito de la pantomima," in *Proceso*, September 1, 1996, pp. 13–17.

12. While Ocampo continues to work at Radio UAG and AFP, he is now also the Chilpancingo correspondent for *La Jornada*.

13. Maribel Gutiérrez is now an editor at *El Sur*, which changed its base to Chilpancingo; Hector Téllez is a photographer with *Milenio* in Mexico City; and Jesús Guerrero is still the *Reforma* correspondent in Chilpancingo.

14. Michael Jordan played for the Chicago Bulls from 1984 to 1993 and then again from 1995 to 1998. During the 1995–1996 season Jordan scored more points than any other player in the National Basketball Association (NBA) and the Bulls won the NBA championship. National Basketball Association: www.nba.com/history/seasonreviews/1995-96/. Accessed January 28, 2018.

THEY TEAR YOU FROM THE WORLD

1. "The blindfold over my eyes has turned me into a defenseless target. Without vision I cannot evade or soften the blows. I sense the blows only as they make impact against me." And: "This becomes a part of the scene of horror: that the torture victim is pulled at by many hands, and that the howls that chill the blood surge from many voices, as if from a pack of hungry wolves. The feeling of being at the mercy of an unknown number of people augments the fear of the torturers." Claudio Tamburrini, *Pase libre: La fuga de la Mansión Seré* (Buenos Aires: Ediciones Continente, 2002), pp. 24 and 65. (All translations from works in Spanish are my own.)

2. Elaine Scarry, *The Body in Pain: The Making and Unmaking of the World* (New York: Oxford University Press, 1985), pp. 29 and 35. The world-destruction of a person is not alien to what is often called "civilization," and it is not the destruction of civilization but rather a hidden part of its roots. As Idelber Avelar writes: "Torture has always entered into the very construction of what is understood and experienced anthropologically as 'civilization,' politically as 'democracy,' and philosophically and juridically as 'truth.' These are concepts whose history is quite indebted to the development of technologies of pain." Idelber Avelar, "From Plato to Pinochet: Torture, Confession, and the History of Truth," in *The Letter of Violence. Essays on Narrative, Ethics and Politics* (New York: Palgrave,

2004), p. 34.

3. Elaine Scarry, *The Body in Pain*, p. 46.

4. "Death is the only way out, I kept telling myself. They have all the time in the world, and you feel that dying is the only way to stop the endless suffering." Nora Strejilevich, *A Single, Numberless Death* (Charlottesville: University of Virginia Press, 2002), p. 15.

5. Nora Strejilevich, "Testimony: Beyond the Language of Truth," *Human Rights Quarterly*, 28(3): p. 702, August 2006.

6. Idelber Avelar, *The Letter of Violence* (New York: Palgrave, 2004), p.31.

7. Marguerite Feitlowitz, *A Lexicon of Terror: Argentina and the Legacies of Torture* (New York: Oxford University Press, revised edition, 2011). The quote reads: "They had so many ways . . . of erasing people, of trying to make you doubt the truth of your own life."

8. See, for example, James Baldwin, *No Name in the Street* (New York: Vintage International, 2007); Silvia Rivera Cusicanqui, *Ch'ixinakax utiwxa. Una reflexión sobre practices y discursos descolonizadores* (Buenos Aires: Tinta Limón, 2010); Michel Foucault, *"Society Must be Defended" Lectures at the College de France 1975-1976* (New York: Picador, 2003); Saidiya V. Hartman, *Scenes of Subjection: Terror, Slavery, and Self-Making in Nineteenth-Century America* (New York: Oxford University Press, 1997), and *Lose Your Mother: A Journey Along the Atlantic Slave Route* (New York: Farrar, Straus, and Giroux, 2007), Achille Mbembe, "Necropolitics" (2003, Public Culture 15 [1]: pp. 11–40); Walter Mignolo, *The Idea of Latin America* (Oxford: Blackwell, 2005); Aníbal Quijano, "Colonialidad del poder, eurocentrismo, y América Latina," in E. Lander, ed., *Colonialidad del saber. Eurocentrismo y ciencias sociales. Perspectivas latinoamericanas* (Buenos Aires: CLACSO Libros, 2005), published in English as Aníbal Quijano, "Coloniality of Power, Eurocentrism, and Social Classification," in Mabel Moraña, Enrique Dussel, and Carlos A. Jáuregui, eds., *Coloniality at Large: Latin America and the Postcolonial Debate* (Durham, NC: Duke University Press, 2008); and Assata Shakur, *Assata: An Autobiography* (Chicago: Lawrence Hill Books, 2001).

9. Tahar Ben Jelloun, *This Blinding Absence of Light* (New York: Penguin, 2006), p. 47. Jelloun's novel is based on the experiences of a survivor of the Tazmamart secret prison in Morocco. The original quote reads: "I realized that dignity was also the refusal to have anything more to do with hope. To survive you had to give up hope. . . . Hope was a lie with sedative properties. To overcome it we had to prepare for the worst

every day. Those who did not understand this sank into a violent and fatal despair."

10. Marguerite Feitlowitz, *A Lexicon of Terror*, pp. 76–77. The complete quotation, with the original emphasis, is as follows: "The physical evidence goes against you, you're so weak, so sick and so tormented you think, if you *can* think: I *am* my shit; I *am* these stinking wounds; I *am* this festering sore. That is what you have to fight. And it's goddamn difficult; because wherever they feel like it, they replenish the physical evidence that goes against you."

11. Mauricio Rosencof, former guerrilla fighter and political prisoner in Uruguay who participated in the mass escape from the Punta Carretas Prison in 1971. The quote is taken from Adrián Pérez, "La fuga de Punta Carretas, una epopeya," in *Página 12*, September 9, 2011.

THE SILENCES

1. See the analysis of the theatricality of the horror carried out by torturers during the Argentine military dictatorship in Marguerite Feitlowitz, *A Lexicon of Terror*.

2. Juliet Cohen, "Errors of Recall and Credibility. Can Omissions and Discrepancies in Successive Statements Reasonably Be Said to Undermine Credibility of Testimony?" *Medico-Legal Journal*, 69 (1): pp. 25–34, 2001.

3. Ibid., p. 11.

4. Quoted in Nora Strejilevich, "Beyond the Language of Truth," *Human Rights Quarterly*, 28 (3): p. 704, August 2006.

5. Strejilevich, "Beyond the Language of Truth," p. 704. See also: Nora Strejilevich, *A Single, Numberless Death* (Charlottesville: University of Virginia Press, 2002).

6. Elaine Scarry writes with power and clarity about how pain breaks language in her book *The Body in Pain*. During an event in Mexico City called "La Guerra de los Dos Lados" (The War on Both Sides) poet Javier Sicilia said the following about the pain he felt on losing a child to murder: "No words can reach it. Language enters a zone of silence." His son, Juan Francisco, and six other people were murdered on March 28, 2011. The other people murdered that day were Julio César Romero Jaimes, Luis Antonio Romero Jaimes, Álvaro Jaimes Avelar, Jaime Gabriel Alejo Cadena, María del Socorro Estrada Hernández, and Jesús Chávez Vázquez.

THE INTERVIEW
1. John Gibler, *Mexico Unconquered*, pp. 231–265.

A PIECE OF BEING
1. Lino Pastoriza, survivor of an accident at sea off the coast of Galicia, cited in Manuel Rivas, *La mano del emigrante* (Alfaguara: Madrid, 2000), pp. 150–151.

WRITING AND VIOLENCE
1. Linda Tuhiwai Smith, *Decolonizing Methodologies: Research and Indigenous Peoples* (London: Zed Books, 2nd edition, 2012), p. 30.

2. Benedict Anderson, *Imagined Communities*, p. 44. Lucien Febvre and Henri-Jean Martin, in their book *The Coming of the Book: The Impact of Printing 1450–1800*, Anderson's source for much of his analysis on print capitalism, write: "We know that by inventing paper the Chinese indirectly contributed to the discovery of printing in Europe. Nothing discovered so far suggests that we owe China any more than that, despite the fact that for nearly five hundred years before Gutenberg the Chinese knew how to print with moveable characters" (p. 71).

3. Anderson, *Imagined Communities*, p. 34.

4. Ibid., pp. 33–34.

5. Ibid., p. 39.

6. Ibid., pp. 38, 39, 42–45.

7. John Beverley, *Testimonio: On the Politics of Truth* (Minneapolis: University of Minnesota Press, 2004), p. 53.

8. Walter Mignolo, *The Darker Side of the Renaissance: Literacy, Territoriality, and Colonization* (Ann Arbor: University of Michigan Press, 2nd edition, 2003), p. 3.

9. Ranajit Guha, *Elementary Aspects of Peasant Insurgency in Colonial India* (Durham, NC: Duke University Press, 1999), p. 52.

10. Janet Duitsman Cornelius, *When I Can Read my Title Clear: Literacy, Slavery and Religion in the Antebellum South* (Columbus: University of South Carolina Press, 1991), p. 66.

11. This denial not only continues, it is not only still constitutive of white supremacy but is the core of an insidious "overrepresentation" of the concept of humanity itself. See *No Humans Involved* and "Unsettling the Coloniality of Being/Power/Truth/Freedom: Towards the Human, After Man, Its Overrepresentation—An Argument," (*CR: The New Centennial Review*, 3 [3]: pp. 257-337, Fall 2003), both by Sylvia Wynter.

No Humans Involved was recently republished as a pamphlet, the publication information for which is as follows: "This pamphlet is one in a series titled On the Blackness of BLACKNUSS, initiated by the Moor's Head Press of BLACKNUSS: books + other relics and published by Publication Studio Hudson. The series is edited by Sharifa Rhodes-Pitts and was begun in the year of Eric Garner, John Crawford III, Mike Brown, Tamir Rice, Cameron Tillman, VonDerrit Myers, Jr., Laquan McDonald, Carey Smith-Viramontes, Jeffrey Holden, Qusean Whitten, Miguel Benton, Dillon McGee, Levi Weaver, Karen Cifuentes, Sergio Ramos, Roshad McIntosh, Diana Showman, and Akai Gurley."

12. José Rabasa, *Writing Violence on the Northern Frontier: The Historiography of Sixteenth-Century New Mexico and Florida and the Legacy of Conquest* (Durham, NC: Duke University Press, 2000), p. 8.

13. Ranajit Guha, "The Prose of Counter-Insurgency" in Ranajit Guha and Gayatri Chakravorty Spivak, *Selected Subaltern Studies* (New York: Oxford University Press, 1988), p. 64.

14. Ranajit Guha, "The Prose of Counter-Insurgency," pp. 64 and 70.

15. Janet Malcolm, *The Journalist and the Murderer* (New York: Vintage Books, 1990), p. 144.

16. Beth Lofredo and Claudia Rankine, "Introduction" to *The Racial Imaginary: Writers on Race in the Life of the Mind* (Albany: Fence Books, 2015), p. 22.

17. Janet Malcolm, *The Journalist and the Murderer*, pp. 3, 142–143.

18. José Rabasa, *Writing Violence on the Northern Frontier*, p. 25.

19. Ibid., p. 22.

20. Ibid., pp. 22–23.

21. I understand Rabasa to be addressing specifically colonial violence. "[D]ecolonization," Frantz Fanon writes, "is always a violent event." Frantz Fanon, *The Wretched of the Earth* (New York: Grove Press, 2004), p. 1.

22. I take this phrase from Walter Mignolo, *The Darker Side of Western Modernity: Global Futures, Decolonial Options* (Durham, NC: Duke University Press, 2011), p. 8. Mignolo writes: "I am stating that the colonial matrix of power is the very foundational structure of Western civilization" (p. 16). Mignolo cites Aníbal Quijano's concept of a "*patrón colonial de poder*" in elaborating his analysis. Quijano writes by way of introduction to his analysis: "What is termed globalization is the culmination of a process that began with the constitution of America and

colonial/modern Eurocentered capitalism as new global powers. One of the fundamental axes of this model of power is the social classification of the world's population around the idea of race, a mental construction that expresses the basic experience of colonial domination and pervades the more important dimensions of global power, including its specific rationality: Eurocentrism. The racial axis has a colonial origin and character, but it has proven to be more durable and stable than the colonialism in whose matrix it was established. Therefore, the model of power that is globally hegemonic today presupposes an element of coloniality." Aníbal Quijano, *Coloniality of Power, Eurocentrism, and Social Classification*, p. 181.

THE SOCIAL WORKER AND THE LAWYER

1. Carlos Montemayor et al., *Diccionario del Náhuatl en el Español de México: Nueva edición corregida y aumentada* (Mexico: Universidad Nacional Autónoma de México and Gobierno del Distrito Federal, 2009).

AN INCREDIBLE ESCAPE

1. Claudio M. Tamburrini, *Pase libre: La fuga de la Mansión Seré* (Buenos Aires: Ediciones Continente, 2002) and Israel Adrián Caetano, *Crónica de una fuga* (K & S Films S.A. and 20th Century Fox, 2006). A transcription of Claudio Tamburrini's official court testimony during the trials of the military dictatorship on June 7, 1985, may be found here: www.desaparecidos.org/nuncamas/web/testimon/tamburrini.htm. Accessed Januray 28, 2018. Antonio Orozco Michel's book *La fuga de Oblatos: Una historia de la LC23 de Septiembre* (Guadalajara: La Casa del Mago, 2007) provides a firsthand account of the seemingly impossible escape of Mexican guerrillas from the Oblatos prison in Guadalajara in 1976.

2. Xavier Montanyá, *La gran evasión: Historia de la fuga de prisión de los últimos exiliados de Pinochet* (Logroño and Barcelona: co-edition, Pepitas de Calabaza and Llaüt, 2009), pp. 117–173.

3. Montanyá, *La gran evasión*, p. 165. The CNI was the Centro Nacional de Informaciones (National Information Center), a State agency of repression, persecution, murder, and forced disappearance active from 1977 to 1990.

4. Luis Carlos Sáinz, *Rejas rotas: Fugas, traición e impunidad en el sistema penitenciario mexicano* (Mexico: Grijalbo, 2013), p. 17.

5. Anabel Hernández, *Los señores del narco* (Mexico: Grijalbo, 2010).

6. Alma Guillermoprieto, "Guzmán: The Buried Truth," *New York*

Review of Books, July 20, 2015: www.nybooks.com/daily/2015/07/20/guzman-escape-extradition-buried-truth/. Accessed January 28, 2018.

7. *El Universal*, "Custodio revela a PGR trama de fuga de reos," May 23, 2009.

8. *El Universal*, "Custodios ayudaron en fuga de reos," September 10, 2010.

9. *El Universal*, "Son 85 los reos fugados de penal en Tamaulipas, September 10, 2010 and *El Universal*, "Cronología Fugas masivas de reos en México," September 17, 2012.

10. Luis Carlos Sáinz, *Rejas rotas*, pp. 245–246.

11. *El Universal*, "Coahuila: se fugan 132 reos de penal," September 18, 2012.

12. *El Universal*, "Reos escaparon por la puerta, no por un túnel," September 19, 2012.

13. Interviews with Ramiro conducted on June 25, 2009, and with Gloria Arenas and Jacobo Silva conducted on September 14, 2010. Ramiro was murdered by paramilitaries on November 4, 2009.

THE BROTHERS

1. Secretaría de Seguridad Pública, Policía Federal Preventiva, Coordinación de Seguridad Regional, Jefatura de Distrito III, Comisaría de Sector 135-XXXI "Orizaba," Parte Informativo de Servicios No. 043/2006, Orizaba, Veracruz, January 12, 2006.

2. Alejandro Jiménez, "Revocan prisión a hermanos de Tzompaxtle," *El Universal*, October 17, 2008, and Emir Olivares Alonso, "Liberan a tres presuntos miembros del EPR por no hallar pruebas en su contra," *La Jornada*, October 19, 2008. While the three men were in jail the EPR published a communiqué declaring that none of the men belonged to their organization. Andrés Tzompaxtle also gave a clandestine press conference and published an open letter stating that the three men did not belong to armed movements. See: "Deslinda el excombatiente Rafael del EPR a sus hermanos de la guerrilla," *El Sur*, April 14, 2006. The PGR carried out a forensic analysis concluding that the handwriting in the notebook did not belong to any of the three imprisoned men.

THE DISAPPEARED

1. Marcela Turati's article about the march (titled "A March with Ten Thousand Absent") begins: "They are the belittled of this administration, the invisible, the mocked, the 'crazy ladies.' They do not rest.

They do not give up despite the years that they have spent going in and out of police stations, where nothing is ever solved. They are looking for their families. . . ." Marcela Turati, "Una marcha con diez mil ausentes," *Proceso*, May 12, 2012.

2. In 2017, the Mexican National Human Rights Commission, a semi-autonomous federal agency, released a report stating that there were 32,236 people reported disappeared and still not located in Mexico between January 1, 2007, and October 31, 2016. (Teresa Moreno, "Registra CNDH 32 mil desaparecidos en México hasta fines de 2016," *El Universal*, April 4, 2017: http://www.eluniversal.com.mx/articulo/nacion/seguridad/2017/04/6/registra-cndh-32-mil-desaparecidos-en-mexico-hasta-fines-de-2016. Accessed January 31, 2018.) This number does not include the estimated tens of thousands of Central Americans disappeared while migrating through Mexico toward the United States over the past ten years. (See: Nina Lakhani, "Mexican kidnappers pile misery on to Central Americans fleeing violence," *The Guardian*, February 21, 2017, www.theguardian.com/global-development/2017/feb/21/mexico-kidnappings-refugees-central-america-immigration, accessed January 31, 2018.) The National Human Rights Commission's figure also does not include estimates of people disappeared whose families did not register formal denunciations with the police, an occurrence all too common when the police are frequently those carrying out the disappearances. In November 2017, the nongovernmental organization Datacívica published an online database with the first and last names of 31,968 people included in the list of the disappeared. (See: datacivica.org.) Over the last six years since this book was originally published in Spanish, I have continued to analyze the terrifying increase in forced disappearances in Mexico as a result of the ongoing "merger" between or "integration" of the State and the transnational illegal drug entrepreneurs, leading to the use of such a particular State form of terror—forced disappearance—now also for mercantile ends. I explored this analysis in "Without Terror, There Is No Business," *NACLA Report on the Americas*, 48 (2): pp. 135–138, Summer 2016; and "Las economías del terror," in Jorge Regalado, ed., *Pensamiento crítico, cosmovisiones, y epistemologías otras para enfrentar la guerra capitalista y construir autonomía* (Gualalajara: Universidad de Guadalajara-CIESAS-Jorge Alonso, 2017), pp. 125–157. My analysis has been greatly influenced by Achille Mbembe's essay "Necropolitics," *Public Culture* 15 (1): pp. 11–40, 2003.

3. Anabel Hernández, "De Calderón a Peña Nieto: los que se

esfumaron," *Proceso*, December 29, 2012.

4. Centro de Derechos Humanos "Fray Francisco de Vitoria, O.P." and Comisión Mexicana para la Defensa y la Promoción de los Derechos Humanos, *Informe sobre desapariciones forzadas en México*. Available at: www.desaparecidos.org/mex/doc/97.htm. Accessed January 28, 2018.

5. Carlos Montemayor, "La Fiscalía Especial" in *La guerrilla recurrente* (Mexico: Debate, 2007), pp. 233–272.

6. Ibid., p. 235.

7. Ibid., pp. 23–236.

ACKNOWLEDGMENTS

Many people helped me while I worked on this book without knowing precisely how they helped me or what I was working on. I'd like to extend to them my heartfelt gratitude: El Carnaval, Suzanna, El Vaquero, Füsun, CRG, La Marx, Emiliano, Mitch, MarieJo, Gloria, Nanea, Amy T, Drew, Jonathan, Pablo, Adriana, Verónica, and Ileana.

For the English edition I would like to also thank with all my heart: Muki, Manni, Charles, Rita, Sorenne and Cormac, Margaret, Suzanne, Ted, Greg, Elaine, Robert, Stacey, and everyone at City Lights.

ABOUT THE AUTHOR

JOHN GIBLER lives and writes in Mexico. He is the author of *Mexico Unconquered: Chronicles of Power and Revolt*, *To Die in Mexico: Dispatches From Inside the Drug War*, *20 poemas para ser leídos en una balacera*, and *I Couldn't Even Imagine that They Would Kill Us: An Oral History of the Attacks Against the Students of Ayotzinapa*.